ما رواه الأساطين في عدم المجيء إلى السلاطين

What The Notables Have Narrated About Not Going To The Rulers

1st Edition

ISBN: 978-0-9567281-0-4

Published by:

Jamiah Media
Email: admin@salafimanhaj.com

Source of translation:

Abridged from *Mā Rawāhu'l-Asātīn fi 'Adm il-Maji ilā's-Salātīn* [What the Notables Have Narrated About Not Going to the Rulers] by Imām Jalāluddīn as-Suyūtī, Abū 'Ali Būsarīh (ed.). Beirut: Dār Ibn Hazm, 1413 AH/1992 CE, pp.5-89.

Cover design & typesetting:

Ihsaan Design - www.ihsaandesign.co.uk

Edited by Abū Fātimah Azhar Majothī

ما رواه الأساطين في عدم المجيء إلى السلاطين

WHAT THE NOTABLES HAVE NARRATED

ABOUT NOT GOING TO THE RULERS

BY IMĀM AL-HĀFIDH

JALĀLUDDĪN AS-SUYŪTĪ (D.911 AH/1505 CE)

Studied and edited by Dr Abū 'Alī Taha Busarīh

Introduced by Shaykh, al-Muhaddith 'AbdulQādir al-Arna'ūt ﷺ

Translated by 'AbdulHaq ibn Kofi ibn Kwesi al-Ashanti

jm JAMIAH MEDIA

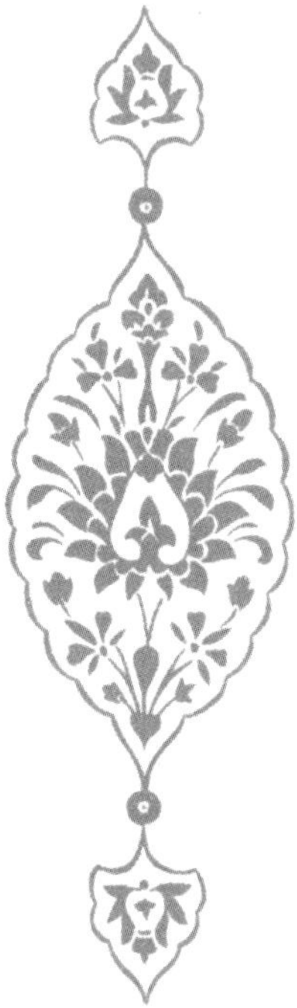

Contents

Translator's Preface....................7

Introduction By The Server Of The Sunnah In Damascus: 'Abdul-Qādir Al-Arnā'ūt....................23

The Virtue Of Knowledge And The 'Ulama: Their Status, Characteristics And Important Qualities....................27

A Mention Of The Views Of The 'Ulama Regarding Entering The Courts And Palaces Of The Rulers....................41

Biography Of Imām As-Suyūtī....................45

Copies Of Manuscript Texts' Used For Editing The Book....................51

The Text [Chapter 1]....................57

Chapter 2....................103

Chapter 3....................121

Bibliography....................146

Jamiah Media Publications....................153

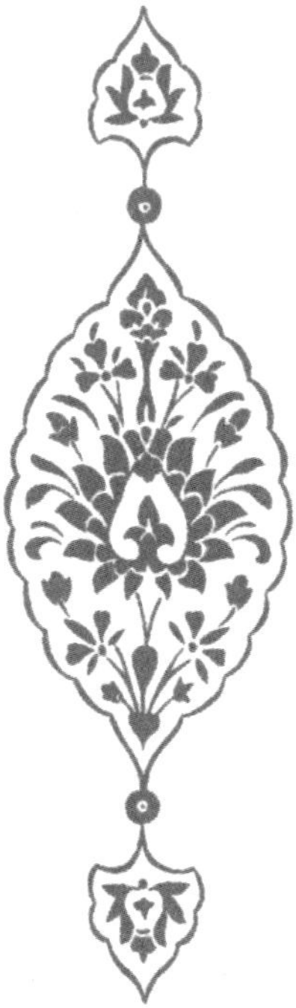

TRANSLATOR'S PREFACE

Indeed, all praise is due to Allāh. We praise Him, we seek His aid, and we ask for His forgiveness. We seek refuge in Allāh from the evil of our actions and from the evil consequences of our actions. Whomever Allāh guides, there is none to misguide him and whoever Allāh misguides, there is none to guide him. I bear witness that there is no god worthy of worship except Allāh and I bear witness that Muhammad is the servant and messenger of Allāh. To proceed:

This is an abridged translation of an important work by Imām Jalāluddīn as-Suyūtī entitled *Mā Rawāhu'l-Asātīn fī 'Adm il-Maji ilā's-Salātīn* [What the Notables Have Narrated About Not Going to the Rulers]. The editor of this work is Dr Abu 'Ali Taha Busarīh who has edited and verified a number of books, such as:

- his Ph.d thesis submitted to *Zaytūnah University* in Tunisia in 1995, *al-Manhaj al-Hadīthī 'inda Ibn Hazm al-Andalūsī* (Dār Ibn Hazm, 2001), it was initially supervised by 'AbdurRahmān 'Awn.
- Abū Muhammad 'AbdulMun'im bin Muhammad bin 'AbdurRahīm bin Muhammad al-Khazrajī al-Ghranātī (aka Ibn ul-Faras, d.597 AH), *Ahkām ul-Qur'ān* (Beirut: Dār Ibn Hazm, 1427 AH/2006 CE).

- Imām al-Hāfidh Abu'l-Hasan Muhammad Ibn ul-Madhfar al-Bazzār (d. 379AH), *Gharā'ib ul-Hadīth Mālik bin Anas* (Dār Gharb ul-Islāmī).
- Abū Muhammad 'AbdulHaq al-Ishbīlī, *al-Jam' Bayna Sahīhayn* (Beirut: Dār ul-Maghrib, 2003, 4 vols.), *tahqīq* with Bashhār 'Awād Ma'rūf.
- 'AbdurRahmān bin Sulaymān bin Maqbūl Ibn Ahdal al-Yemeni, *Ahkām ul-'Azā'im wa'r-Raqā* (Beirut: Dār Ibn Hazm, 1417 AH/1997 CE).
- 'Abdullāh bin Muhammad al-Batalyawsī, *Mushkilāt Muwatta' Mālik bin Anas* (Beirut: Dār Ibn Hazm, 1420 AH).
- Imām Muhammad at-Tāhir ibn 'Āshūr (d.1394 AH), *Kashf ul-Mughtī min al-Ma'āni wa Alfādh al-Wāqi'ah fi'l-Muwatta'* (Tunisia: Dār Sahnūn, 1427 AH/2006 CE).
- Muhammad al-Misnāwī bin al-Mālikī al-Fāsī (d. 1136 AH), *Nusrat ul-Qabdh wa Radd 'ala man Inkara Mashrū'iyyatahi fi Salāt il-Fard* (Beirut: Dār Ibn Hazm, 2007), *tahqīq* with 'AbdulLatīf bin al-Imām Bū 'Azīzī.

The importance of this topic cannot be denied for a number of reasons, including the Salaf's dislike of pandering to the desires of the corrupt oppressive and transgressive rulers. Sufyān ath-Thawrī ﷺ stated for example:

> "I do not fear the punishment of the rulers, rather I fear the honour of the rulers."[1]

At the same time though, the Salaf did not rebuke those pious leaders who tried their utmost to implement Islām and in fact these leaders are praised and held in high regard. For this reason, many scholars also authored works wherein they extolled the virtues of the 'Ulama remaining close to the rulers. For example, Abu'l-Hasan 'Ali bin Muhammad bin Habīb al-Māwardī (d. 450 AH) authored *Nasīhat ul-Mulūk*; Abū Hāmid al-Ghazālī (d. 505 AH) authored *at-Tibr al-Masbūk fī Nasīhat ul-Mulūk*; Abū Bakr Muhammad bin al-Walīd at-Tartūshī (d. 520 AH) authored *Sirāj ul-Mulūk*; Ibn ul-Jawzī (d. 597 AH), for example authored *'Atf ul-'Ulama 'ala Umarā' wa'l-Umarā' 'ala'l-'Ulama* [The Scholars Connection to the Leaders and the Leaders to the Scholars], which was written well over three hundred years prior to as-Suyūtī's book; Mulā 'Ali Qārī (d.1014 AH/1606 CE) authored *Tab'īd ul-'Ulama 'an Taqrīb il-Umara'* [Distancing the Scholars from Proximity to the Rulers]; Imām Muhammad bin Ismā'īl as-San'ānī (d. 1182 AH) authored *Izālat ut-Tuhmah bi Bayān mā Yajūz wa Yuhram min Mukhālat idh-Dhalamah* [Removing the Accusation by Explaining What is Permitted and Prohibited from Mixing with the Oppressors]. Imām

---

[1] Reported by Abu'sh-Shaykh al-Asfahānī in *Tabaqāt ul-Muhaddithīn bi Asbahān* (Beirut: Mu'assasat ur-Risālah, 1412 AH/1992 CE) vol.2, p.114, 219; Abū Nu'aym, *Hilyat ul-Awliyā'*, vol.10, p.390; adh-Dhahabī, *Siyar A'lām un-Nubalā'*, vol.7, p.262.

Muhammad bin 'Ali bin Muhammad bin 'Abdullāh ash-Shawkānī (d. 1250 AH) authored *Raf' ul-Asātīn fī Hukm il-Ittisāl bi's-Salātīn* [Raising of the Notables Regarding the Ruling of Being Connected to the Rulers].

Some scholars have stated that the ruler represents the dominion while the scholar represents the deen hence 'Ali ibn Abī Tālib ﷺ stated:

> "The dominion (mulk) and the deen are two brothers, one is not sufficed from the other. The deen is the foundation and the dominion is the protector, and whatever has no foundation is destroyed and whatever has no protector is lost."[1]

This link is seen as being the complete connection between the pen and the sword, as one scholar of the past said to a leader: "we are in the shade of your sword" and the leader replied to the scholar: "and we are in the shade of your pen!"[2] Ibn ul-Jawzī ﷺ also mentioned three types of rulers who the 'Ulama should have some kind of relationship with, and to what extent:

> **First:** the just ruler who follows the truth, supporting him is an obligation and frequenting him is an act of worship.

---

[1] Ibn 'AbdulBarr, *Bahjat ul-Majālis*, vol.1, p.332.

[2] This statement was ascribed to Fakhr ar-Rāzī to the Sultān Shihābuddīn Muhammad bin Sālim al-Ghūrī, refer to Ibn Hajar al-'Asqalānī, *Lisān ul-Mīzān*, vol.4, p.420.

Second: the ruler who does some things correctly and some things incorrectly, such a ruler has to be alerted and reminded based on his extent of accepting the truth. He should be written to in a kind way and matters should be indicated to him.

Third: the ruler who is most oppressive and is rarely correct. I have explained the extent that such a ruler should be rejected and if possible this should be with gentleness and if this is not possible then one should stay away from such a ruler, and if this is possible, it is the better course of action.[1]

Ibn Muflih al-Maqdisī ﷺ stated in his book *al-Ādāb ush-Shar'iyyah*, in a section entitled *Inqibād ul-'Ulama al-Muttaqīn min Ityān il-Umarā' wa's-Salātīn* [The Pious Scholars' Restriction from Going to the Rulers and Leaders], edited by Dr Muhammad 'Ali al-Marsafī:

> Imām Ahmad ﷺ did not go to the Khulafā', rulers or princes and prevented writing to them and completely forbade his companions from that. This has been transmitted from him by a group (of scholars) and his words in regards to this is well known... this was the

[1] 'AbdurRahmān bin 'Ali bin al-Jawzī (d. 597 AH), *'Atf ul-'Ulama 'ala'l-Umarā' wa'l-Umarā' ala'l-'Ulama* [The Connection of the Scholars to the Leaders and of the Leaders to the Scholars]. Riyādh, KSA: 1427 AH/2006 CE, ed. Ibrāhīm Bājis 'AbdulMajīd, p.45.

> view of a group of the Salaf and their words in regards to that are also well known... yet a group of other scholars from the Salaf opposed them in this view.

Then Ibn Muflih stated:

> What is evident is that there is a dislike if it is feared that one will fall into prohibitions; but if one can stay away from harm and achieve a benefit over the fear of them, and can admonish them and fulfil a worthy need, it is recommended. Based upon these conditions the words and actions of the Salaf are to be applied, may Allāh be pleased with them. As for the just ruler, then going to him and supporting him in his justice is of the most glorious types of closeness. As 'Urwah bin az-Zubayr, Ibn Shihāb and their generational level who were of the best of 'Ulama used to accompany 'Umar bin 'Abdul'Azīz. Ash-Sha'bī, Qabīsah bin Dhu'ayb, al-Hasan, Abu'z-Zinād, Mālik, al-Awzā'ī and ash-Shāfi'ī ﷺ used to visit the ruler. In any case, it is safer to cut off from them as chosen by Ahmad and many other 'Ulama.

Then Ibn Muflih relayed some ahādīth and narrations warning against going to the rulers and leaders. As-San'ānī stated in his *Izālat ut-Tuhmah bi Bayān mā Yajūz wa Yuhram min Mukhālat idh-Dhalamah* [Removing the

Accusation by Explaining What is Permitted and Prohibited from Mixing with the Oppressors]:

Mixing with oppressors is of various types: that which necessitates an abundant reward and that which necessitates a painful torment. The first type involves explaining to the leader what is obligatory on him, guiding him and teaching him knowledge of the Sharee'ah, and even if he does not act in accordance to what is being mentioned to him, the Sharee'ah has been conveyed and this is obligatory by agreement. This type of mixing (with oppressors) is obligatory by agreement and includes the mixing of Allāh's Messengers with the disbelievers and those who Allāh applied 'dhulm' on, Allāh says:

﴿ وَٱلْكَـٰفِرُونَ هُمُ ٱلظَّـٰلِمُونَ ﴾

"The disbelievers - they are the wrongdoers [*Dhālimūn*]"

{al-Baqara (2): 254}

It is well known that every Messenger of Allāh mixed with the disbelievers, visited them and sat with them in order to instruct them to īmān and forbid them from kufr and disobedience so that they would become close to ar-Rahmān and distant from ash-Shaytān. This is obligatory on every scholar as they are the inheritors of the Messengers during every time and this is instructing the good and forbidding the evil which is obligatory on every person as verified by the texts of the Qur'ān and Sunnah.

Second type: that one mixes with them (the transgressors) out of fear of the oppressor's evil towards himself, wealth and honour. This is permissible and could even be obligatory, Allāh says:

﴿ إِلَّآ أَن تَتَّقُوا۟ مِنْهُمْ تُقَىٰةً ﴾

"...except when taking precaution against them in prudence"

{Āli 'Imrān (3): 28}

This is in regards to the disbelievers, thus an oppressive Muslim has more preference in regards to this.

Third type: mixing with an oppressor who is a relative, this is permitted and there is no blame for this, as Allāh says in regards to the disbelieving parents:

﴿ وَصَاحِبْهُمَا فِى ٱلدُّنْيَا مَعْرُوفًا ﴾

"...but accompany them in [this] world with appropriate kindness..." *{Luqman (31): 15}*

Fourth type: mixing with them (the transgressors and oppressors) for worldly interaction such as buying and selling, this is permitted by agreement of the scholars. This is as long as he knows, or thinks, that what the oppressor has is not harām. The jurists have discussed this matter and have said: "It is allowed to deal with an oppressor, in terms of buying and selling, in that which is not thought to be prohibited. As there is no trade except by mixing and the proof of this is the consensus of the Companions and their business dealings with Jews and other disbelievers. Indeed, our Messenger ﷺ died and his sword was pawned to a Jew and they are of the most oppressive people as you have heard in the Qur'anic verse."

Fifth type: mixing with oppressors in order to take from their wealth which is your right anyway, this is permitted and was done by the Imāms of Islām.

The types of permitted association with oppressors are many and they are not prohibited by consensus and agreement of the scholars; except for mixing with oppressors in order to help them in their oppression of taking the wealth and property of Allāh's worshippers and shedding their blood out of transgression. Whoever mixes with them to aid them in such void actions and supports them via his speech, weapons, pen, treatment or tacit approval is like them in disobeying Allāh and thus sinful. There is a threat and punishment relayed for this type of interaction.

Then as-San'ānī relayed the ahādīth in regards to warning against going to the oppressive rulers and supporting them in their oppression. Imām Muhammad bin Sālih al-'Uthaymīn رحمه الله, one of the contemporary scholars who passed away in the last ten years, stated in his commentary to Imām ash-Shawkānī's book *Raf' ul-Asātīn*:

The scholars' connection with the rulers is split into three categories:

First: in order to instruct them to good and forbid them from evil, and aiding them in implementing Allāh's Sharee'ah. This is regardless of whether the scholar is a judge or a Muftī, or one who instructs good and forbids evil.

Second: whoever aids the rulers in their oppression and could even be a liar who says about the people "they are doing this" and "they are doing that" and there is no doubt that such a person is associated with them in oppression and could even be more oppressive in that he indicates to such rulers things which are not true.

Third: the one who has a neutral position and goes to the leaders in order to be close to them and makes the leaders pleased and becomes familiar with them and speaks about unnecessary matters sometimes. We can possibly say that his not going is better than his going and we could also say that his going is better than his not going as if he goes, and he is known for knowledge, or the leaders know that he is from Ahl ul-'Ilm, the leaders will become acquainted with Ahl ul-'Ilm and the leaders will not flee from them even if this contains no good in guiding the leader or preventing him from oppression. If the scholar leaves them the leaders will flee from Ahl ul-'Ilm and say: "Ahl ul-'Ilm do not show us anything while the common people come to us from their markets and sit with us while those scholars do not sit with us" – this will lead to distance (between the leaders and the scholars).[1]

When there developed a trusted relationship between the leaders and their scholars, the leaders brought the scholars close to them as righteous associates. These scholars, and many others, viewed the link with the rulers as being based on the necessity for it and on any interest derived from it in accordance with the Divine Legislation. However, some scholars warned to the utmost degree against going to the rulers and leaders; from those who dedicated an entire book to the subject, which is this book between our hands now, was Imām Jalāluddīn as-Suyūtī (d. 911 AH/1505 CE) and this work is: *Mā Rawāhu'l-Asātīn fī 'Adm il-Maji ilā's-Salātīn* [What the Notables Have Narrated About Not Going to the Rulers].

In this work, as-Suyūtī relays many statements from the *'Ulama* warning against being near to the rulers and leaders, to the extent that there are few narrations that he relays regarding the importance of advising the rulers. Furthermore, some of the ahādīth that are used by some of the contemporary Khawārij of the era, as mentioned within as-Suyūtī's book, are not only *da'īf* but also do not support *takfīr* of the rulers, revolt and assassination attempts! So as we shall see, even though the Salaf greatly

---

[1] Shaykh Muhammad bin Sālih al-'Uthaymīn, *at-Ta'līq 'ala Risālah: Raf' ul-Asātīn fī Hukm al-Ittisāl bi's-Salātīn* (Riyadh, KSA: Dār ul-Watan, 1430 AH), ftn.1, 18-19.

disliked going to see rulers, leaders, kings and their officials, at the same time the Salaf did not call to: speaking bad about the rulers from the pulpits and minbars; *takfīr* of the rulers; fighting the rulers; assassinating the rulers and all-out rebellion and coup attempts against the corrupted transgressing oppressive rulers. Abu'l-Walīd at-Tartūshī stated in *Sirāt ul-Mulūk*:

> None hopes for the removal of the ruler except a misguided ignoramus or a vile sinner who hopes for all kinds of prohibited things. The duty on the ruled is that they hope that Allāh rectifies the ruler, that advice is given to him and that supplication for the ruler to be rectified is made. This is because within the ruler's rectification is rectification for the servants and the lands and within his corruption is corruption of the servants and the lands.[1]

Ibrāhīm Bājis 'AbdulMajīd stated in his critical edit *(tahqīq)* of Ibn ul-Jawzī's *'Atf ul-'Ulama 'ala Umarā' wa'l-Umarā' 'ala'l-'Ulama*:

> Advising the leaders of the people is obligatory according to the Shar' [Divine Legislation] and decisive according to the intellect. If the rulers have any evil within them, who will be the ones who forbid them and work to remove such evil?[2]

---

[1] Abu'l-Walīd at-Tartūshī, *Sirāt ul-Mulūk*, p.157.

[2] 'AbdurRahmān bin 'Ali bin al-Jawzī (d. 597 AH), *'Atf ul-'Ulama 'ala'l-Umarā' wa'l-Umarā' ala'l-'Ulama* [The Connection of the Scholars to the Leaders and of the

The answer no doubt is: the 'Ulama, hence Sufyān ath-Thawrī ﵀ stated:

> "None is to command the ruler to good except for a man who has knowledge of what he is commanding to, has knowledge of what he is forbidding, is gentle when commanding, gentle when forbidding, just when commanding and just when forbidding."[1]

An example of this type of deception, false reasoning and error can be seen in an article from a *takfīrī* website which, after listing the statements of the Salaf regarding staying away from the leaders, proceeds to then make a ruling that rulers are apostates and have to be fought against!? Hereby trying to link the statements of the *Salaf* regarding staying away from the rulers to the revolutionary antics of the *khawārij*.[2] Moreover, Dr Muhammad bin 'Abdillāh al-Mas'arī (head of the London-based *CDLR*), the Saudi dissident who uses absolutely anything he can lay his hands on to criticise the rulers, reels off *da'īf hadīth* after *da'īf hadīth* in his book *Muhāsabat ul-Hukkām* (1418 AH/1997 CE) with no checking or

---

Leaders to the Scholars]. Ibrāhīm Bājis 'AbdulMajīd (ed.). Riyādh, KSA: 1427 AH/2006 CE, p.12.

[1] Abū Nu'aym, *Hilyat ul-Awliyā'*, vol.6, p.379.

[2] See:
http://sayyidoon.wordpress.com/2008/03/26/115%E2%80%9Cscholars%E2%80%9D-that-befriend-tyrants/
Also here: http://islamicsystem.blogspot.com/2007/07/various-ahadīth-about-rulers.html

verification whatsoever.[1] However, our Shaykh and teacher, 'AbdusSalām bin Burjis Āl 'AbdulKarīm[2] ﷺ stated in his valuable work *Qat' ul-Mira' fī Hukm id-Dukhūl 'ala'l-Umarā'* [Cutting off the Dispute Regarding the Ruling of Visiting the Rulers]:

---

[1] The book can be seen here and from pages 6-22 are the evidence for his lack of verification:
wisnusudibjo.files.wordpress.com/2008/03/fiqh-muhasabah-al-hukam.doc

[2] Our Shaykh ﷺ died in 2004 in a car accident while travelling back from Qatar to Saudi, the Shaykh was in his late thirties. We were with the Shaykh the week prior to the accident and we prayed over him at the Muftī's Masjid in Riyadh and many of the 'Ulama were at the Janāzah such as the Muftī, 'Abdul'Azīz Aali Shaykh, Ma'ālī Sālih Āli Shaykh and many other scholars, students and notables, may Allāh preserve them. The Shaykh ﷺ visited Brixton Mosque in London [Masjid Ibn Taymiyyah] on many occasions from the mid 1990s onwards. At Brixton in 2003, he delivered a number of beneficial lectures, lessons and question and answer sessions and some of these audios are available for download at: www.salafimanhaj.com. The Shaykhs teachers include: Imams Bin Baz and Uthaymīn and Shaykhs Ibn Jibrīn, Abdullāh ad-Duwaysh, Sālih al-Atram, Abdullāh al-Qu'ūd, Abdullāh al-Ghudayyān, AbdulKarīm al-Khudayr and many others. The Shaykh was a Qādī in Riyadh and authored over twenty five books and critically edited and studied over 20 works by the Hanbali scholars of Najd, such as: *Tārīkh Tadwīn al-'Aqīdah as-Salafiyyah* [The History of the Codification of the Salafi Creed]; *Mu'amalat ul-Hukkām* [Dealing with the Rulers]; *al-Ahādīth an-Nabawiyyah fī Dhamm il-'Unsuriyyah il-Jāhiliyyah* [Prophetic Hadīths Censuring Racism], introduced by al-'Allāmah Sālih al-Fawzān; *al-Qawl ul-Mubīn fī Hukm il-Istihzā bi'l-Muminīn* [The Clear Word on the Ruling of Mocking the Believers], introduced by Imam Uthaymīn, etc.

Attention: the immense dislike of the Salaf of visiting the kings and princes does not mean the permissibility of revolting against them or supporting disobeying them – by the praise of Allah, this is clear with the people of knowledge and the students.

Shaykh 'AbdusSalām Burjis ﷺ also states:

> We have comprehended our scholars, who were truthful advisors, such as Shaykh 'Abdul'Azīz bin Bāz and Shaykh 'Abdullāh bin Humayd, visiting their kings as truthful advisors. This was also the case for those 'Ulama before them such as Shaykh Muhammad bin Ibrāhīm Āli Shaykh, Shaykh Sa'd bin 'Atīq, Shaykh Sulaymān bin Sahmān, Shaykh 'Abdullāh bin 'Abdul'Azīz al-'Anqarī. Likewise is the case for the rest of the 'Ulama of the da'wah, may Allāh have mercy on them all.[1]

I hope that the noble reader will find benefit in this effort and that Allāh will place it in my scale of good deeds.

'AbdulHaq ibn Kofi ibn Kwesi al-Ashanti
Stockwell, South London (UK)
Dhu'l-Qa'dah 1431 AH/October 2010 CE

---

[1] See pp.75-79

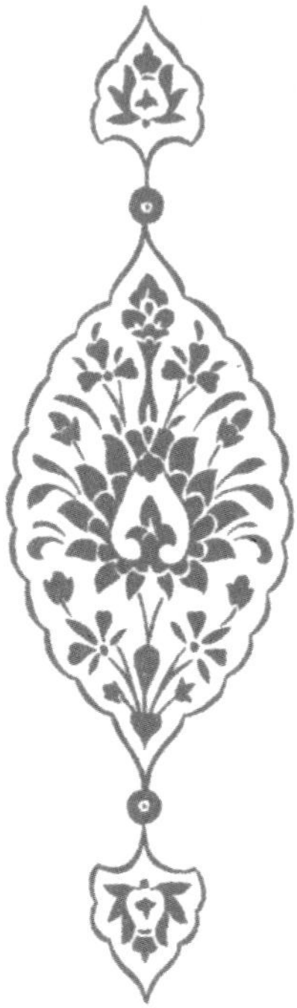

INTRODUCTION BY THE SERVER OF THE SUNNAH IN DAMASCUS: 'ABDULQĀDIR AL-ARNA'ŪT

Indeed, all praise is due to Allāh. We praise Him, we seek His aid, and we ask for His forgiveness. We seek refuge in Allāh from the evil of our actions and from the evil consequences of our actions. Whomever Allāh guides, there is none to misguide him and whoever Allāh misguides, there is none to guide him. I bear witness that there is no god worthy of worship except Allāh and I bear witness that Muhammad is the servant and messenger of Allāh. To proceed:

We are in a time wherein we are in need of understanding what the *'Ulama* and luminaries have mentioned in regards to not going to the (palaces and courts of the) leaders and rulers out of fear of being put to test by them by their worldly things. The intent of this is nothing but commanding the good and forbidding vice, along with abstaining from what the leaders have in their hands. Our brother for the sake of Allāh, Ustādh Abū 'Ali Taha Būsarīh at-Tūnisī *(hafidhahullāh)* has investigated what has been written in regards to this subject and has compiled a treatise based on the work of Imām as-Suyūtī ﷺ entitled *Mā Rawāhu'l-Asātīn fī 'Adm il-Maji ilā's-Salātīn* [What the Luminaries Have Narrated About Not Going to the Rulers]. He based this on two manuscript copies of the original text by Imām as-Suyūtī and compared the two manuscripts and explained the differences between the two. Ustādh Abū 'Ali Būsarīh also wrote the sources of the hadīth, the numbers of the verses of the Qur'ān and verified the Prophetic ahādīth with an academic verification utilising source referencing of those ahadith to the sources of those ahādīth. He has also transmitted what the *'Ulama* of hadīth have mentioned in regards to those ahādīth based on the *qawā'id* (principles) of *mustalah* (hadīth terminology) and according to what was said by the *'Ulama* of *Jarh wa't-Ta'dīl* regarding some individuals who have been transmitted from in certain hadīth. Likewise, Ustādh Abū 'Ali Būsarīh has also checked most of the narrations that the author (Imām as-Suyūtī ﷺ) mentioned and along with this explained the ahādīth based upon what the distinguished *'Ulama* of hadīth have noted. He has also explained some of the strange words via referral to the famous linguistic compilations and has provided biographies of some of the notables mentioned in the treatise just as he has mentioned the biography of Imām as-Suyūtī (the author of the treatise) in his introduction.

We are in great need of the likes of this treatise during this era wherein many *'Ulama* frequent the gates of the kings, leaders and rulers hoping to benefit from the worldly things that they possess. The Messenger of Allāh ﷺ informed about the likes of these when he said: *"Whoever goes to the gates of the ruler has been tested"*, for a slave (of Allāh) does not get any closer to a ruler in order to profit from his worldly things except that he has become further away from Allāh. Whoever assists a ruler in his *dhulm* (oppression) is not truly from the Ummah of Muhammad ﷺ and whoever frequents them and takes from their dunya has actually taken more from his own deen, but whoever stays away from the rulers is safe and whoever mingles with them is destroyed. The *'Ulama* of the past from the Sahābah, the Tābi'īn and their followers abstained from what the rulers and leaders had in their hands and if they entered (their courts or palaces), they would command them to good and forbid them evil, along with exhorting them to fear Allāh by referring to the verses of the Qur'ān and the Prophetic ahādīth about their responsibilities over their people. For instance, they would mention to the rulers the saying of the Prophet ﷺ for example: *"Each of you is a shepherd and each is responsible for his flock."* The kings and leaders would listen to the advice given to them because they knew that those *'Ulama* did not want any money from them, rather they wanted to absolve themselves from responsibility with Allāh.

The editor of this treatise, may Allāh preserve and protect him, has mentioned the stories between the *'Ulama* and the rulers and how the *'Ulama* were honoured and respected with Allāh and with the people. They explained to the leaders that the scholar is to be visited and does not visit (rulers) and that the scholar has to be come to and does not go (to see rulers). Al-Hasan al-Basrī ﷺ said,

> ...withhold your hands from the blood of the Muslims, withhold your stomachs from the wealth of the Muslims and withhold your tongues from (speaking about) their honours. Do not sit with *Ahl ul-Bida'* (the people of innovation) and do not go to the kings who will corrupt your deen.

Sufyān ath-Thawrī ﷺ said similar to this. Salamah bin Dīnār said,

> In the past, if the leaders sent someone to fetch the 'Ulama, the 'Ulama would not go to them, or if the rulers asked the 'Ulama, the 'Ulama would not make any concessions for them. The rulers would go to the 'Ulama at their houses and ask them there and within this was rectification for both the rulers and the 'Ulama.

Sufyān ath-Thawrī said:

> Knowledge will remain honoured until it is carried to the gates of the kings who take it for a small price, then Allāh will remove the sweetness (of knowledge) from their hearts.

All of this indicates the *fitan* and *fasād* that is within the *'Ulama* mingling with the kings, rulers and leaders if they intend (obtaining) their dunya, for whoever supplicates for an oppressor to remain has loved to disobey Allāh within His earth. So the student of knowledge has to look at the biographies of those glorious *'Ulama* in order to take their actions as an example.

The author of this treatise is al-Hāfidh as-Suyūtī; he was pure, kind, righteous, pious and observant of his sustenance. The wealthy leaders would come and visit him and present wealth to him which he would reject. Towards the end of his life, he secluded himself away in his homes and occupied himself with knowledge and authoring until he was afflicted with an illness which ended with his death in 911 AH (1505 CE) ﷺ. May Allāh reward the editor of this work with the best of rewards and increase him in success in order to produce more of the likes of these valuable treatises from the books of the Sunnah which are a light and blessing for the Muslims. We ask Allāh, the Most Blessed, to make this work sincerely for His Noble Countenance and our last supplication is that all praise is due to Allāh, the Lord of the Worlds.

Written by,
'AbdulQādir al-Arna'ūt
The Server of the Sunnah in Damascus
1 Rajab 1411 AH (16 January 1991 CE)
Damascus

THE VIRTUE OF KNOWLEDGE AND THE 'ULAMA: THEIR STATUS, CHARACTERISTICS AND IMPORTANT QUALITIES

Indeed, all praise is due to Allāh. We praise Him, we seek His aid, and we ask for His forgiveness. We seek refuge in Allāh from the evil of our actions and from the evil consequences of our actions. Whomever Allāh guides, there is none to misguide him and whoever Allāh misguides, there is none to guide him. I bear witness that there is no god worthy of worship except Allāh and I bear witness that Muhammad is the servant and messenger of Allāh. To proceed:

Allāh has elevated the affair of the *'Ulama* and has mentioned their affair and indicated this, He says in His Clear Revelation,

﴿ يَرْفَعِ ٱللَّهُ ٱلَّذِينَ ءَامَنُوا۟ مِنكُمْ وَٱلَّذِينَ أُوتُوا۟ ٱلْعِلْمَ دَرَجَـٰتٍ ﴾

"Allāh will raise those who have believed among you and those who were given knowledge, by degrees." *{al-Mujādilah (58): 11}*

﴿ قُلْ هَلْ يَسْتَوِى ٱلَّذِينَ يَعْلَمُونَ وَٱلَّذِينَ لَا يَعْلَمُونَ ﴾

"Say, "Are those who know equal to those who do not know?"" *{az-Zumar (39): 9}*

﴿ يُؤْتِى ٱلْحِكْمَةَ مَن يَشَآءُ ۚ وَمَن يُؤْتَ ٱلْحِكْمَةَ فَقَدْ أُوتِىَ خَيْرًا كَثِيرًا ۗ
وَمَا يَذَّكَّرُ إِلَّآ أُو۟لُوا۟ ٱلْأَلْبَـٰبِ ﴾

"He gives wisdom to whom He wills, and whoever has been given wisdom has certainly been given much good. And none will remember except those of understanding." *{Baqarah (2): 269}*

Just as the Messenger of Allāh ﷺ explained the respect and nobility that Allāh has promised for the *'Ulama* in this life and the next. In *Sahīh Muslim* from the *hadīth* of Abū Hurayrah ﷺ in *marfū'* form,[1] that *"Whoever embarks on a way in order to obtain knowledge, Allāh will ease his way to Paradise."* In the hadīth of Abu'd-Dardā' ﷺ which is reported by Abū Dāwūd, at-Tirmidhī, Ibn Mājah, Ibn Hibbān in his *Sahīh* and al-Bayhaqī in his *ash-Shu'b*: *"Indeed the angels spread out their wings over the student of knowledge out of pleasure from what the student has done. They ask for forgiveness of the scholar in the heavens and in the earth and even the fish in the waters seek forgiveness for him. The virtue of the scholar over the worshipper is like the virtue of the moon over all of the stars, for the 'Ulama are the inheritors of the Prophets. The Prophets neither bequeath the dīnār nor the dirham rather they bequeath knowledge. So whoever takes hold of it has acquired a great fortune."* At-Tirmidhī reported from a hadīth of Abū Umāma al-Bāhilī ﷺ that he said: the Messenger of Allāh ﷺ mentioned two men: one who was a

---

[1] A *marfū' hadīth* is a narration which is ascribed to the nabi ﷺ and contains either his speech, an action, a tacit approval, his physical features or mannerisms. There are also times when statement of a companions takes the ruling of being *marfū'*, such as when one of them mentions a matter which they could not possibly have known except by way of the Prophet. [TN]

worshipper and the other who was a scholar, he then mentioned who had more virtue, *"The virtue of the scholar over the worshipper is like the virtue of me over the least of you..."* Abū 'Īsā at-Tirmidhī said "the hadīth is hasan sahīh." Allāh with His Blessing and Virtue set a great reward and an elevated status for the sincere scholar which does not cease in this life, let alone in the afterlife. It has been authenticated from the Prophet ﷺ from the *hadīth* of Abū Hurayrah in *marfū'* form that: *"When the son of Ādam dies his actions cease except for three: some charity that he gave, some beneficial knowledge that he left or a righteous son who makes dua'a for him."* It is found in the *Sahīh* of Muslim.

Allāh specified the *'Ulama* over the rest of the believers and favoured them, teaching them the Book and the *Hikma* and giving them understanding of the *deen* and of the correct interpretations. So Allāh favoured them over the rest of the believers throughout all times and epochs. He raised them with knowledge and adorned them with *hilm*. By them (the *'Ulama*), the *halāl* is known from the *harām*, the *haq* is known from the *bātil*, the beneficial is known from the harmful, and the good from the bad. Their virtue is great and so is their (potential) danger. They are the inheritors of the Prophets and the coolness of the eyes of the Righteous. Even the fish in the sea seek forgiveness for them and the angels spread out their wings over them in humility. On the Day of Judgement, the *'Ulama* will be after the Prophets in intercession. Their gatherings bring wisdom and their actions admonish the people who are heedless. They are the most virtuous of the servants and they have the highest station of the *zuhhād*. Their lives are enriched and their deaths are a calamity. They remind the heedless and they teach the ignorant. With their good manners they humble the defamers and with the beauty of their admonishment they bring back the negligent. All of their knowledge is needed and the correct (answers) to those who oppose them are also needed, obeying them with all good characteristics is obligatory and disobeying them is a sin. Whoever obeys them is guided and whoever disobeys them has been stubborn. They are the torch of the servants *('ibād)* and the light of the lands *(bilād)*, and they are responsible for the Ummah. They bring about wisdom, they resist Shaytān and they cause the hearts of the people of truth to be enlivened and the hearts of the people of deviation to die. Their likeness in the earth is like the stars in the heavens which are used as guides in the darkness of the land and at sea...[1]

Allāh obligated those who carry knowledge to benefit others with what they have learnt. Allāh in more than one verse dispraised the *yahūd* for carrying knowledge without benefiting others with that knowledge. From what Allāh mentioned wisely was,

[1] From the words of Imām al-Ājurrī in his valuable book *Akhlāq ul-'Ulama*, pp.33-35.

﴿ مَثَلُ ٱلَّذِينَ حُمِّلُوا۟ ٱلتَّوْرَىٰةَ ثُمَّ لَمْ يَحْمِلُوهَا كَمَثَلِ ٱلْحِمَارِ يَحْمِلُ أَسْفَارًۢا ۚ
بِئْسَ مَثَلُ ٱلْقَوْمِ ٱلَّذِينَ كَذَّبُوا۟ بِـَٔايَـٰتِ ٱللَّهِ ۚ وَٱللَّهُ لَا يَهْدِى ٱلْقَوْمَ ٱلظَّـٰلِمِينَ ﴾

"The example of those who were entrusted with the Torah and then did not take it on is like that of a donkey who carries volumes [of books]." *{Al-Jumu'ah (62): 5}*

In the same way, it has been authenticated from the Prophet ﷺ from the *hadīth* of Abū Hurayrah, as reported by Abū Dāwūd, an-Nasā'ī, Ibn Mājah and al-Hākim, that he said: *"O Allāh I seek refuge in you from four: from knowledge which does not benefit, from a heart that does not fear, from a soul which is not satisfied and from a supplication which is not heard."*[1]

Al-Hāfidh Ibn Hibbān al-Bustī said:

> The intelligent one does not occupy himself with seeking knowledge unless he intends to act according to it, because whoever strives in other than what we have described only increases in pride and arrogance, wasting and leaving (good) action. So his corruption could affect others more so than corrupting his own self, rendering himself as Allāh has said,

﴿ لِيَحْمِلُوٓا۟ أَوْزَارَهُمْ كَامِلَةً يَوْمَ ٱلْقِيَـٰمَةِ ۙ وَمِنْ أَوْزَارِ ٱلَّذِينَ يُضِلُّونَهُم بِغَيْرِ
عِلْمٍ ۗ أَلَا سَآءَ مَا يَزِرُونَ ﴾

---

[1] Al-Hākim declared it Sahīh and adh-Dhahabī agreed.

"...and some of the burdens of those whom they misguide without knowledge. Unquestionably, evil is that which they bear." *{an-Nahl (16): 25}*[1]

Then Allāh mentions it as being the most obligatory spread and conveyance of knowledge to the people when He mentioned in His Clear Revelation,

﴿ وَإِذْ أَخَذَ ٱللَّهُ مِيثَٰقَ ٱلَّذِينَ أُوتُوا۟ ٱلْكِتَٰبَ لَتُبَيِّنُنَّهُۥ لِلنَّاسِ وَلَا تَكْتُمُونَهُۥ
فَنَبَذُوهُ وَرَآءَ ظُهُورِهِمْ وَٱشْتَرَوْا۟ بِهِۦ ثَمَنًا قَلِيلًا ۖ فَبِئْسَ مَا يَشْتَرُونَ ﴾

"And [mention, O Muhammad], when Allāh took a covenant from those who were given the Scripture, [saying], "You must make it clear to the people and not conceal it."

{Āli-'Imrān (3): 187}

Al-Hāfidh Ibn Kathīr ad-Dimishqī ﷺ stated in his *tafsīr*:

> This is a chastisement from Allāh and a threat to the people of the scripture...also within this is a caution to the 'Ulama not to traverse their way (i.e. the way of the people of the scripture) and then be afflicted as they were and not follow the way that they did. The *'Ulama* have to use that beneficial knowledge which is in their hands which lead to righteous actions, and they are not to hide anything...[2]

---

[1] *Rawdat ul-'Uqalā*, p.35

[2] Ibn Kathīr, *Tafsīr al-Qur'ān al-'Adhīm*, vol.1, p.347

What the Islamic Ummah is in need of today are *'Ulama* who comprehend the responsibility of knowledge and teach the importance that rests on their necks due to it in this life. The classifier of *Sirāj ul-'Ibād wa Manār il-Bilād* stated:

> Those who were bedazzled by the material development of the 20th century forgot their own heritage and forgot that they were the best Ummah in existence due to an important distinction – which is that they command to good and forbid the evil, yet before this they have *īmān* in Allāh,
>
> ﴿ كُنتُمْ خَيْرَ أُمَّةٍ أُخْرِجَتْ لِلنَّاسِ تَأْمُرُونَ بِٱلْمَعْرُوفِ وَتَنْهَوْنَ عَنِ ٱلْمُنكَرِ وَتُؤْمِنُونَ بِٱللَّهِ ﴾
>
> **"You are the best nation produced [as an example] for mankind. You enjoin what is right and forbid what is wrong and believe in Allāh."** ***{Āli-'Imrān (3): 110}***
>
> Evil and *bātil* does not raise its head except with the sleeping of the people of truth and those who command to good. Evil and *bātil* do not find any avenue in the reality of life except when the *'Ulama* abandon their importance and that time understandings change, the scales are turned, the truth is confused with falsehood and commanding good is confused with commanding evil. This is what

we live through and we feel its effects within our societies which are established upon other than the guidance of Allāh.[1]

From the most affirmed obligations on the people of knowledge, for which there is more reward, is for them to teach the people and spread the beneficial knowledge that Allāh has placed within their hearts. The *hadīth* of the Prophet ﷺ narrated by Zayd bin Thābit in *marfū'* form and reported by Ibn Hibbān in his *Sahīh* bears testimony to this: *"There are three things which should not leave the heart of a Muslim: sincere action for Allāh, advising the people in authority and adhering to the Jama'ah. Whoever makes the dunyā his main aim, then Allāh will place poverty between his eyes and he will not achieve that of the dunyā except that which is written for him. Whoever makes the Hereafter as his main aim Allāh will bring his affair together and place his riches in his heart and the dunya will come to him submissively."*[2]

Many ahādīth have been relayed which severely forbid hiding knowledge as is mentioned in the famous hadīth of Abū Hurayrah ؓ which has been reported by Abū Dāwūd, at-Tirmidhī (who graded it hasan), Ibn Mājah and authenticated by al-Hākim according to the conditions of the latter two, in *marfū'* form, *"Whoever is asked about knowledge (that he knows*

---

[1] From the introduction to the book by Imām al-Ājurrī, Dr Fārūq Hamādah (ed.), *Akhlāq ul-'Ulama*, pp.24-25.

[2] See *Sahīh at-Targhīb*, no.85

about) and hides it will be bridled on the Day of Judgement by a bridle of fire."[1]

From the most dangerous of sins which affect a person and lead to destruction in the Hereafter, is the lack of *ikhlās* (sincerity) in seeking knowledge. The first thing that one studying should give importance to and make his main aim is the ruin of the *dunya* and its ephemeral scraps. The student should be mindful of the punishment without taking into account the reward that Allāh possesses on the Day of Judgement. What testifies to this is the hadīth of Abū Hurayrah in *marfū* form: *"Whoever learns knowledge which is sought for Allāh's Countenance but does not learn it except for a worldly intent, will not find the scent of Paradise on the day of Judgement."*[2] Reported by Ahmad, Abū Dāwūd and Ibn Mājah. So the intelligent one does not sell his fortune of the Hereafter with what he has intended by seeking knowledge due to the ruin of the dunya that will be obtained by doing this.[3] Then Allāh cautions against approaching the wicked oppressive leaders and the sinful rebels by saying,

﴿ وَلَا تَرْكَنُوٓا۟ إِلَى ٱلَّذِينَ ظَلَمُوا۟ فَتَمَسَّكُمُ ٱلنَّارُ ﴾

"And do not incline toward those who do wrong, lest you be touched by the Fire..." *{Hūd (11): 113}*

---

[1] Ibid., no.116

[2] Al-Khatīb at-Tibrīzī, *Mishkāt ul-Masābīh*, no.227, authenticated by al-Albānī.

[3] Ibn Hibbān, *Rawdat ul-'Uqalā'*, p.34

Not to mention co-operating with them and waiting at their doors, so then how about granting concessions to those rulers and issuing *fatāwā* for their own benefit yet contravene the Divine Upright Islamic Legislation?

> Thus, the people of knowledge have to safeguard their knowledge from being a means to despicable aims and lowly ends and flattering the rulers, because this is humiliating that which Allāh has honoured (i.e. knowledge) and lowering it from its elevated position. How beautiful is the saying of Sufyān ibn 'Uyaynah, "I was given the understanding of the Qur'ān, but when I accepted money from Abū Ja'far I was deprived of that understanding. We ask Allāh for forgiveness."[1]

I say: from the most beautiful things that I have come across in this issue is the extremely precious speech of the major cultivator of the *manhaj* of the *Salaf us-Sālih*, the Hāfidh, Imām Abū Bakr Muhammad bin al-Husayn al-Ājurrī ﷺ. I will transmit some of it for the respected reader and I recommend referring to the book for the rest of what the Imām mentions in his beneficial book *Akhlāq ul-'Ulamā*. It is a unique book in its subject-matter as al-Hāfidh Ibn Rajab al-Hanbalī ﷺ highlighted. Imām al-Ājurrī

---

[1] From Dr Fārūq Hamādah's introduction to *Akhlāq ul-'Ulama*, p.28 by Imām al-Ājurrī.

noted, after mentioning the censured manners of those who Allāh has not benefitted with their knowledge:

> These characteristics and the likes can overpower the heart of the one whose knowledge does not benefit. These characteristics therefore manifest if his soul loves nobility and position, loves sitting with the kings and the children of the dunya, loves to associate with them due to their pleasing standard with splendid houses and means of travel, servants, fine clothes, comfortable beds and tasty appetizing food. Such a (scholar) also loves people who visit his door, listen to his words and obey his orders. He is not able to do any of this except via being in the position of adjudication (judgement), so he seeks this position (of being a judge) and this is not possible for him to do unless he has surrendered his deen and humbled himself to the kings, their followers and their aides. So he serves himself over to them and even gives over his wealth to them. (Such a scholar) will also keep quiet about the manifest filth that occurs due to their evil within their homes, sayings and actions. Then, (such a scholar) will begin to beautify many disgusting things and exalt them based on his incorrect false interpretation, all in order to make himself look good to them (rulers). So when (this scholar) does this over a long period of time and corruption has become ingrained into him, they (the rulers or kings) appoint him to assume a position of adjudication (like a judge) and this is in fact slaughtering the scholar but without

a knife! In this way, the scholar owes a great favour to them and he has to express his thanks to them (for giving him that position), therefore he goes to great lengths so as not to anger them which will result in them removing him from that position. Yet he is not bothered about angering his Kind Lord so he embezzles the wealth of the orphans, widows, the poor, the needy, the monies given for *wuqūf* (religious endowments), the wealth which is supposed to be for the Mujāhidīn, the nobles (Ahl ush-Sharaf) of the Haramayn and the wealth that is meant to be for all of the Muslims to benefit from. However, he (such a scholar) uses this wealth for his clerk, chamberlain and servant! So he eats of the harām, feeds off the harām and thus, the evidence against him is increased. So woe betide the one whose knowledge bequeaths such characteristics. This is a scholar who the Prophet ﷺ sought refuge from and ordered refuge to be sought from. This is a scholar about whom the Prophet ﷺ said, *"The people who will face the most severe punishment on the Day of Judgement is the scholar whose knowledge did not benefit him."*[1]

---

[1] *Ahklāq ul-'Ulama*, pp.138-141. The hadīth is reported by at-Tabarānī in *al-Mu'jam as-Saghīr* and by others and it is very *da'īf* (*jiddan*), see al-Albānī, *ad-Da'īf ul-Jāmi' as-Saghīr*, no.868.

[TN] The hadīth is *da'īf jiddan* due to Abū Salamah 'Uthmān bin Miqsam al-Burrī al-Kindī al-Basrī being in the *isnad*, Yahyā ibn Ma'īn said about him "'Uthmān al-Burrī is nothing! He is well-known for lying and fabricating hadīth." Ibn al-

How beneficial is what was said by the Imām, al-Hāfidh, al-Hujjah, al-'Allāmat ul-Andalus, Abū Muhammad bin Hazm when he advised the 'Ālim in his treatise *Marātib ul-'Ulūm*:

> To be afflicted by associating with the Sultān (leader) is to be afflicted by a great calamity and it is presenting oneself to a vile danger in which one's deen and self will depart. (The scholar) is not to associate with him (i.e. the ruler) whatsoever as this will lead to ruin and to be ruined on account of an oppressed praiseworthy person who will be rewarded is better than being ruined due to an oppressive evil sinful and dispraised person remaining. It may be that his destruction will be swift or it may be delayed. But whatever the case there is no escape from ruin. So one should know that if the Sultān (leader) sees from him (i.e. the scholar) any tenderness on his deen and advises him in regards to that which does not affect his provisions, then he increases his trust in that scholar and is glorified in his eyes. But if, on the other hand, he (the ruler) sees him (the scholar) as covetous and affecting his immediate interests over his Hereafter then he has a bad opinion of him and does not trust him

---

Mubārak said: "He was a Qadarī, and much of what he relays is unknown." Mentioned in *al-Mīzān* by Imām adh-Dhahabī. Al-Juzajānī also accused 'Uthmān al-Burrī for lying and Yahyā al-Qattān, an-Nasā'ī and ad-Dāraqutnī all left him and did not report from him. It is reported by ad-Dārimī (vol.1, p.82) with an authentic *isnad* but as being a saying of Abu'd-Dardā' ﷺ. For more see Imam Ibn Hajar, al-*Lisān*, vol.4, p.155 and Imam al-Albānī, *Silsilah ad-Da'īfah*, vol.4, p.138.

> with regards to his own self, this is if he sees that he (the scholar) has a share in bringing about his (the ruler's) destruction.[1]

This is the speech of a scholar who assisted many states of the world and their dangers and he has life-long experience of adverse circumstances and what comes with that. Ibn Hazm ﷺ had the most knowledge of the people in regards to the manners of the kings and their characteristics.[2] So take his advice because despite its brevity it is very beneficial, *inshā'Allāh.*

---

[1] Dr Ihsān 'Abbās (ed.), *Majmū' ar-Rasāil Ibn Hazm al-Andalūsī*, vol.4, p.76.

[2] Hopefully Allāh will make it easy for me to complete my academic paper on Ibn Hazm's hadīth methodology, indeed Allāh is the Supporter of success.

A MENTION OF THE VIEWS OF THE 'ULAMA REGARDING ENTERING THE COURTS AND PALACES OF THE RULERS

I view that it is important that I mention three points around this issue:

Firstly: What the majority of the Salaf viewed in their forbiddance of frequenting the gates of the rulers and staying away from them, al-Hāfidh Ibn Rajab al-Hanbalī ﷺ said:

> Many of the Salaf used to forbid entering the courts and palaces of kings and also for those who wanted to command them to good and forbid them from evil. From those who forbade this were 'Umar ibn 'Abdul'Azīz, Ibn al-Mubārak, ath-Thawrī and other Imāms...the reason for this was out of fear of the tribulation that comes with entering (the courts or palaces of) the rulers.[1]

---

[1] *Sharh hadīth "Mā Dhi'bān Jā'i'ān"*, published in the margins of *al-Jāmi'*, vol.1, pp.216-218 by Ibn 'AbdulBarr.

[TN] For an English translation of the above reference by Ibn Rajab al-Hanbalī see: Ibn Rajab al-Hanbalī, Badr 'Abdullāh al-Badr (ed.), Abū Talhah Dāwūd Burbank (trans.), *The Evil Craving for Wealth and Status* (Birmingham: Al-Hidāyah, 1995), p.30.

Then Ibn Rajab ﷺ explained this with what has been mentioned prior from al-Ājurrī and what has been mentioned in this book by Imām as-Suyūtī ﷺ within his indexing of the statements of the Salaf regarding this forbiddance.

Secondly: That there is a dislike of visiting the rulers which is the view of al-Hāfidh, az-Zāhid, al-Wā'idh, al-Murabbī al-Kabīr, Ibn Rajab al-Hanbalī and this appears in his following words:

> From this matter also is that it is disliked to visit kings and approach them, for this is a door from which the 'Ulama of the dunya enter in order to achieve nobility and positions.[1]

Thirdly: That it is permissible to visit them as long as this is limited and restricted to certain conditions which are according to the view of some of the Salaf and Khalaf, and was the view of Mālik ﷺ and was also a view supported by the Imām of al-Maghrib Ibn 'AbdulBarr an-Nimarī al-Andalūsī when he said:

> It was said to Imām Mālik: "You visit the leader while they oppress and transgress? May Allāh have mercy on you! Where is the one

---

[1] *Sharh hadīth "Mā Dhi'bān Jā'i'ān"*, published in the margins of *al-Jāmi'*, vol.1, pp.216-218 by Ibn 'AbdulBarr.

speaking the truth?!"[1] Imām Mālik said "It is the right of every Muslim or man that Allāh has made in his heart some knowledge and *fiqh* to go to the Sultān and command him to good, forbid him from evil and admonish him until it is clear to him that a scholar has entered his presence rather than someone else. As the scholar only enters (the courts and palaces of) the rulers in order to command him to good and forbid him from evil, so if it is for this reason then this is a virtue after which there is not virtue.[2]

The Imām of hadīth and *fiqh* in al-Maghṛib during his day, Abū 'Umar bin 'AbdulBarr ﷺ, may Allāh make Paradise his reward, said, after transmitting much in the way of ahādīth and narrations forbidding going to the rulers:

> All of this is in regards to the oppressive sinful ruler, but as for the just ruler who is virtuous then he should be visited, seen and supported upon righteousness which is the most virtuous action of goodness. Do you not see that 'Umar bin 'Abdul'Azīz only had the upright '*Ulama* accompany him? The likes of 'Urwah bin az-Zubayr, Ibn Shihāb (az-Zuhrī) and others of that generational level. Ibn Shihāb (az-Zuhrī) used to eṇter (the court of) 'AbdulMālik and his sons after him. From those who also used to visit the courts of the

---

[1] Verified by Ibn Abī Hātim in *al-Jarh wa't-Ta'dīl*, vol.1, p.30 and the similar is to be found in Qādi 'Iyyād, *Tartīb ul-Madārik*, vol.1, p.207.

[2] Ibid.

rulers were: ash-Sha'bī, Qabīsah, Ibn Dhu'ayb, Rajā' bin Haywah al-Kindī, Abu'l-Miqdām (who was a virtuous scholar), al-Hasan, Abu'z-Zinād, Mālik bin Anas, al-Awzā'ī, ash-Shāfi'ī and a group (of scholars) which would be lengthy if all were mentioned.[1] If a scholar is present with a ruler, depending on there being a need to do that, and says good and speaks with *'ilm* then this is good and seeking Allāh's Pleasure on the Day of Meeting. However, such a gathering (of the scholar and the ruler) is a fitnah in most occasions and leaving such gatherings is safer.[2]

---

[1] So pay attention! [TN]

[2] Ibn 'AbdulBarr, *Jāmi' Bayān ul-'Ilm wa Fadlihi*, vol.1, p.227

BIOGRAPHY OF IMĀM AS-SUYŪTĪ

HIS NAME, ASCRIPTION AND BIRTH

He is 'AbdurRahmān bin Abī Bakr bin Muhammad bin Sābiq al-Khudayrī, as-Suyūtī, nicknamed "Jalāluddīn", Abu'l-Fadl.He was born in 849 AH and was raised as an orphan in Cairo after his father died when he was five years old. He memorised the Qur'ān when he was less than eight years old and then he memorised *al-'Umdah, Minhāj ul-Fiqh wa'l-Usūl, Alfiyyah Ibn Mālik* and then preoccupied himself with *'ilm*.

HIS SHAYKHS AND TRAVELS

He took *fiqh* and *nahw* (Arabic grammar) from a group of Shuyūkh and studied the *farā'id* from the 'Allāmah of the topic of his era, Shaykh Shihāb ud-Dīn ash-Shār. He also read the Sharh of *al-Majmū'* with him. Imām as-Suyūtī also remained close to Shaykh ul-Islām 'Ilmuddīn al-Balqīnī and studied *fiqh* with him until the Shaykh died after which Imām as-Suyūtī remained close to the son of al-Balqīnī and he gave as-Suyūtī *ijāzah* to teach and give *fatāwa*, this was in the year 876 AH (i.e. Imām as-Suyūtī was 27 years old at the time). Imām as-Suyūtī also remained close to Shaykh Sharafuddīn al-Munāwī and benefited from him in *fiqh* and *tafsīr*. He read hadīth and Arabic language with the Shaykh, Imām Taqiuddīn ash-Shiblī al-Hanafī who wrote some commendations for as-Suyūtī. Imām as-Suyūtī also attended the gatherings of al-'Allāmah al-Kāfijī for fourteen years and gained from him the arts of *tafsīr, usūl* and meanings and he gave as-Suyūtī *ijāzah*. In the same way, Imām as-Suyūtī benefited from the lessons of Sayfuddīn al-Hanafī in *tafsīr* and *balāgha*. The number of Shuyūkh that gave him ijāzah, and to whom he read and heard from are 51, as he himself compiled as did his student ad-Dāwadī who arranged the names of his teachers alphabetically. Shaykh as-Suyūtī travelled to Shām (the Levant), Hijāz (Western Arabia), al-Yemen, Hind (India), Maghrib (Morocco), Takrūr (which is Chad)[1] and then finally settled in Misr (Egypt).

HIS MANNERS

---

[1] [TN]: Dr Abū 'Ali Busarīh refers to this place as being "Takrūrī" which is incorrect as the area was actually known as "Takrūr" in Arabic, nor did it refer to Chad, but rather the Senegal Valley and where the Senegalese and Mauritanian border is currently located. It was an empire which flourished from 800-1285 CE and was a rival with the ancient Empire of Ghana. It embraced Islam in the 11th Century CE and may have sided with the Berber Almoravids (al-Murabitun) against the Ancient Kingdom of Ghana, which was located in what is now South-Eastern Mauritania, Western Mali and Eastern Senegal. It thus appears that the term "Takrūr" by the time of as-Suyūtī was a generic term for West Africa. See Umar al-Naqar, "Takrur the History of a Name", *The Journal of African History*, Vol. 10, No. 3 (1969), pp. 365-374. For more on this in relation to Imām as-Suyūtī see: M. Sartain, "Jalal al-Din as-Suyūtī's Relations with the People of Takrur," *Journal of Semitic Studies*, vol.16, no.2 (1971), 193-198. Also refer to the following article by John Hunwick on Imām as-Suyūtī's meeting with Askiya Muhammad Toure (1442 - 1538 CE), the Soninke king of the Songhai Empire, in the journal *Sudanic Africa*, vol.2, (1991): http://www.hf.uib.no/smi/sa/2Askiya.html

He was pure, kind, righteous, pious and observant of his *rizq*, the rulers and the wealthy would travel to him to visit him and present precious wealth to him and he would reject it. There was none like him to be seen during his time. He called for *ijtihād* and at times was frank about this yet at other times merely suggested it.[1] This led him to have serious problems with some of his contemporaries who accused him of certain things,[2] especially al-Hāfidh as-Sakhāwī. It reached the extent that each of them authored writings against each other, the issue is well known.[3]

HIS WORKS

Imām as-Suyūtī is well known for his abundant writings within all arts of the Islamic heritage, especially in regards to hadīth, *tafsīr, fiqh* and *usūl.* However, from his works are those which vary between the size of just a page to voluminous works. The first book that he authored was *Sharh ul-Isti'ādhah wa'l-Basmalah* in the year 866 AH and he was seventeen years old at the time of writing it. What he mainly did within these books was to gather from various books and summarise well what he read, his good chaptering also indicated his great mind.

---

[1] Muhammad Lutfī as-Sabbāgh, *Muqaddimat Tahdhīr ul-Khuwās*, p.36

[2] As Sakhāwī, *ad-Daw' ul-Lawāmi'*, vol.4, p.65

[3] See ash-Shawkānī, *al-Badr ut-Tāli'*, vol.1, pp.328-335; Muhammad Lutfī as-Sabbāgh, *Muqaddimat Tahdhīr ul-Khuwās*, p.42-47.

There are also a number of small writings that as-Suyūtī authored which follow what was widespread during his time such as some Sufi ideas which are not correct and there is no doubt that these particular writings conform with what was common and thus as-Suyūtī found for them *Shari'* justifications for what they had written and heard. Such as, the belief that Khidr is alive now, the use of the *subhah* (beads), affirming the existence of *abdāl*[1] and *aqtāb*[2] and the likes.[3]

I say: contradictions, confusion, slip-ups and academic errors are sometimes to be found within these many writings, which sometimes result from hastiness in authoring, a lack of source-referral and a lack of verification, as

---

[1] This is a Sufi term that they apply to "substitutes" and there are a number of fabricated *ahādīth* regarding the *abdāl*. Abū Rumaysah from the UK has authored a beneficial research paper in English assessing the *ahādīth* that are used and found that they were all *da'īf* and fabricated. The main scholars of hadīth throughout the centuries have ruled such hadīth regarding the so-called "abdāl" to be utterly weak and fabricated. The paper by Abu Rumaysah can be referred to here: http://almuttaqoon.com/index.php?showtopic=265 [TN]

[2] This is a Sūfī term which refers to Sufi "poles" or "axis" who the Sufis assign superhuman qualities, some of which are attributes which in Islam are only assigned to Allāh. [TN]

[3] From the introduction to the book *Tahdhīr ul-Khuwās*, p.51 by Ustādh as-Sabāgh.

has been noticed by all who conduct work on as-Suyūtī's writings, as some editors have documented.[1]

From the best of what he authored was *Husn ul-Muhādharah, Tadrīb ur-Rāwī, al-Itqān fī 'Ulūm il-Qur'ān, al-Mazhar fī 'Ulūm il-Lughah, Hamu' ul-Hawāmi'* and other works, to the extent that his works which have been published from his classifications number 250 books.

HIS STUDENTS

From the most famous students of Imām as-Suyūtī, then it is possible to say that the most prominent graduates from the school of as-Suyūtī was the historian Imām ad-Dāwadī (d. 945 AH) the author of *Tabaqāt ul-Mufassirīn* and other works. Also the famous historian Ibn Iyyās the author of *Bidā'i' uz-Zuhūr* (d. 930 AH). Also the Imām, al-Hāfidh Ibn Tūlūn al-Hanafī (d. 935 AH), the author of *al-Fahāris* and of many other works. Likewise of his students was Imām ash-Sha'rānī the author of *at-Tabaqāt* who died in 973 AH.

HIS SICKNESS AND DEATH

[1] See Ahmad bin as-Siddeeq al-Ghumārī, *al-Mughīr fī'l-Ahādīth al-Mawdū'ah fī'l-Jāmi as-Saghīr*, pp.5-8; the introduction of al-Albānī to *Sahīh* and *Da'īf ul-Jāmi' as-Saghīr* and *Ahādīth ad-Da'īfah.*

As-Suyūtī stayed away from the people and secluded himself in his house occupying himself with knowledge, research and authoring up until he fell ill with a sickness which went on for seven days and ended with his death. That was in Jumadā al-Awwal 911 AH (October 1505 CE), may Allāh have mercy on him.[1]

---

[1] For the biography of Imām as-Suyūtī see:

As-Suyūtī, *Husn ul-Muhādharah*, vol.1, p.335

As-Sakhāwī, *ad-Daw' ul-Lāmi'*, vol.4, p.65

Najmuddeen al-Ghazzī, *al-Kawākib as-Sā'irah fi A'yān al-Mi'at il-'Āshirah*, vol.1, p.226

Ibn ul-Iyyās, *Bida'i' uz-Zuhūr*, vol.4, p.83

Ibn ul-'Imād al-Hanbalī, *Shadharāt udh-Dhahab*, vol.8, p.51

Ash-Shawkānī, *al-Badr ut-Tāli'*, vol.1, p.328

Siddeeq Hasan Khān, *at-Tāj ul-Mukallal*, p.349

Khayruddeen az-Ziriklī, *al-I'lām*, vol.4, p.71

'Umar Ridā Kahālah, *Mu'jam ul-Mu'aliffeen*, vol.5, p.128

COPIES OF MANUSCRIPT TEXTS' USED FOR EDITING THE BOOK

I relied on two written copies for this critical edition:

First copy: It is found within a compilation of other manuscripts and numbered 11527 at the *Maktabah al-Ahmadiyyah,* the printing house of *Dār ul-Kutub al-Wataniyyah* in Tunisia. It is written on the back of the copy that it was drafted during the 10th Islamic century AH. It is written in a clear Eastern (Arabic) script and is 13.5 by 18 centimetres and each page has between 19 and 20 lines. The book begins on page 17 (of the manuscript copy) and ends on page 29. On the margins of the manuscript are some commentaries and topics which indicate the attention and knowledge of the copyist. At the end of the compilation it is mentioned: "al-Mubārak Mūsā bin Ahmad Zafiyāwī came across this book and it was written out by Mūsā bin Ahmad Ibrāhīm Zafiyāwī, may Allāh forgive him and his parents, Āmeen." When I mention this manuscript copy of the book I refer to it with the letter 'a' (manuscript 'a').

Second copy: This is also to be found within a compilation of manuscripts at the *Maktabah al-Ahmadiyyah* in Tunisia and is numbered 11328. The book of as-Suyūtī is found between folio no.154/b up to folio 160/b and its size is 29.5 by 19.5 centimetres and there are 38 lines per page. It is written in the clear Maghribi script and it features some important words in red ink such as: "Al-Bukhārī reported in *at-Tārīkh*...and I say.....". This indicates that it began with a hadīth which shows the thinking of the author. Towards the end of the document it is mentioned: "...on Monday 11 Safar 1057 AH." The author of this compilation was Muhammad bin at-Tayyib "az-Zayn" or "al-Wazīr" as due to the smallness of the letters it was not clear to me what his name said. When I mention this manuscript copy of the book I refer to it with the letter 'b' (manuscript 'b').

Due to the preciousness of this book, and the importance of its subject-matter, a body of *'Ulama* have referred to it, such as Shaykh Murtada az-Zabīdī who used a fair portion of the book within his *Sharh* of *Ihyā 'Ulūm ud-Dīn*[1] and likewise the historian Najmuddīn al-Ghazzī also metrically composed it and appended some additions to it,[2] in a number of instances Shaykh al-'Ajlūnī refers to it in his book *Kashf ul-Khafā'*.[3]

ASCRIBING THE BOOK TO IMĀM AS-SUYŪTĪ

Some of those who have written biographies of as-Suyūtī mention the book, such as al-Ghazzī in *al-Kawākib us-Sā'irah*,[4] this in turn was used by az-

---

[1] *Ithāf us-Sādat il-Muttaqīn*, vol.6, pp.124-145

[2] *Al-Kawākib us-Sā'irah*, vol.1, p.228

[3] Vol.2, p.249

[4] Vol.1, p.228

Zabīdī and al-'Ajlūnī as has preceded and was mentioned by the author of the book *Maktabat ul-Jalāl as-Suyūtī.*[1] The book (*Mā Rawāhu al-Asātīn*) in its content and style certifies that the book is ascribed to Jalāl as-Suyūtī, to the extent that there is no room for doubt. As-Suyūtī himself indicates to the existence of the book in an abridgement of it which is still in manuscript form.[2]

THE METHOD OF VERIFICATION

a. I compared the two manuscript copies and explained some of the differences between the two, in the notes I have indicated any discrepancies in each of them.

b. I have checked the *ayāt* and numbered them.

c. I have academically checked and clearly verified the Prophetic ahādīth used and I have graded every hadīth in order to clarify the authentic from the weak hadīth where possible. I have also relayed the full chains of transmission and discussed these chains based on the statements of the Imāms of *Jarh wa't-Ta'dīl* and via referral to the views of scholars of hadīth of the past who gave rulings on those ahādīth.

---

[1] Dr Ahmad ash-Sharqāwī

[2] *Ar-Risālah as-Sultāniyyah*, a copy within a set of manuscripts in the *Maktabah al-Wataniyyah* [National Library] in Tunisia, numbered '8863'.

d. I have verified most of the narrations mentioned by the author in the book, if I do not find the narration in the source that as-Suyūtī ﷺ has referred to then I have explained another source where the narration can be located.

e. I have explained some of the ahādīth based on what the explainers of hadīth have mentioned. In the same way I have explained any strange words based on what the dictionaries state. I have safeguarded brevity in that and applied vowelization of words where necessary.

f. I have added an introduction which speaks about the virtue of *'ilm* and the *'Ulama* in Islam and I conducted a brief study regarding the issue of going to the rulers. I presented the views of the majority of the Imāms regarding the issue and I also presented a brief biography of as-Suyūtī. I also placed various academic indexes at the end of this edit, research and study.

g. The respected Shaykh, al-'Allāmah, al-Muhaddith, al-Faqīh 'AbdulQādir al-Arna'ūt *(hafidhahullāh)* reviewed this work, may Allāh make him benefit the Muslims and reward him with good.

Finally I hope from Allāh that He makes this work sincere for His Noble Countenance and for it to benefit the believers, and may all praise be due to Allāh firstly and lastly.

Pictures From The Manuscripts

Opening page from manuscript (a)

Closing page from manuscript (a)

Opening page from manuscript (b)

Closing page from manuscript (b)

THE TEXT

بسم الله الرحمن الرحيم

In the name of Allāh, the Most Beneficent, the Most Merciful,

This is *Mā Rawāhu'l-Asātīn fi 'Adm il-Maji ilā's-Salātīn* [What the Notables Have Narrated About Not Going to the Rulers]:

Abū Dāwūd reported,[1] as did at-Tirmidhī who graded the hadīth as being *hasan*,[2] an-Nasā'ī[3] and al-Bayhaqī in *Sh'ub ul-Īmān*[4] from Ibn 'Abbās رضي الله عنهما from the Prophet ﷺ who said:

---

[1] In *Kitāb us-Sayd* [Book of Hunting], *Chapter on Constantly Following Hunting*, vol.3, p.111, no.2859 and at the end of it "Whoever goes to the Sultān is tested."

[2] *Kitāb ul-Fitan*, chapter no.69, vol.4, p.523, hadīth no.2256 with the like wording of Abū Dāwūd who said at the end: "in the chapter the hadīth is transmitted from Abū Hurayrah and this hadīth is *hasan sahīh* from the hadīth of Ibn 'Abbās. We do not know the hadīth except via ath-Thawrī."

[3] In *Kitāb us-Sayd wa'dh-Dhibā'ih, Chapter on Constantly Hunting*, vol.7, pp.195-196 with the same wording as the other two (Abū Dāwūd and at-Tirmidhī).

[4] With the wording *"whoever is attached to hunting is heedless..."* and the rest of the instances when the hadīth is mentioned with this wording. He said: "Yahyā bin Sālih was the only one to report it with his isnad", vol.7, p.47, hadīth no.9402. As-Sakhāwī in *al-Maqāsid ul-Hasanah*, no.1132 ascribed the hadīth to al-Bayhaqī.

«من سكن البادية جفا، ومن اتبع الصيد غفل، ومن أتى أبواب السلاطين افتتن»

"Whoever lives in the desert becomes harsh, whoever preoccupies himself with following hunting becomes heedless and whoever goes to the doors of the rulers is tested."[1]

---

[1] I say: The hadīth has been reported from Ibn 'Abbās via various routes such as: Ahmad in *al-Musnad*, vol.1, p.537; Abū Nu'aym in *Hilyat ul-Awliyā*, vol.4, p.72; al-Bayhaqī in *Sunan al-Kubrā*, vol.10, p.101; Ibn 'AbdulBarr in *Jāmi' Bayān ul-'Ilm wa Fadlihi*, vol.1, p.198; Ibn 'AbdulBarr via Wakī' with the wording "*whoever lives in the desert becomes harsh and whoever constantly goes hunting becomes heedless.*" Adh-Dhahabī relayed the hadīth in *Siyar 'A'lām un-Nubalā'*, vol.4, p.552 and said: "Abū Mūsā is majhūl". Shaykh Shu'ayb al-Arna'ūt said in the *ta'līq* that: "Abū Mūsā is majhūl but the rest of the men in the chain are thiqāt and it has supporting from the hadīth of Abū Hurayrah with Ahmad in his *Musnad*, vol.2, p.371 and its *sanad* is *hasan*." Adh-Dhahabī said in *Mīzān ul-'I'tidāl*, vol.4, p.578: Shaykh Yamānī is unknown and none relayed from him except ath-Thawrī, and he is possibly Isrā'īl bin Mūsā who is *majhūl* and al-Hāfidh Ibn Hajar indicated his jahālah in *Taqrīb ut-Tahdhīb*, vol.2, p.479. Ustādh as-Sabbāgh says in his commentary on *Mukhtasar al-Maqāsid il-Hasanah* (by az-Zurqānī), vo.1038, transmitting from al-Munāwī (who mentioned in *Fayd ul-Qadīr*, vol.6, p.153): "the hadīth is reported from four, including Abū Mūsā who is not known at all." Al-'Allāmah al-Mubārakfūrī said in *Tuhfat ul-Ahwadhī*, vol.6, pp.532-533: *"Whoever lives in the desert becomes harsh"* means: "becomes ignorant", for Allāh says,

"The bedouins are stronger in disbelief and hypocrisy and more likely not to know the limits of what [laws] Allāh has revealed to His Messenger."

{at-Tawbah (9): 97}

Al-Qārī and al-Qādī said:

'Jafā ar-Rajulu' ("the man became harsh") if he becomes hard-hearted and harsh and has neither tenderness nor goodness to his relatives. This is the condition of most of those who live in the desert regions due to their distance from the people of knowledge and also due to their lack of mingling with the people. As a result, their nature becomes that of wild animals. *"Whoever hunts constantly becomes heedless"* means he adhered to hunting and preoccupied himself with it, and becomes occupied with play and music. As for the word "heedless" then it means to be heedless from obedience, worship and adhering to the Jama'āh, in this way the person becomes akin to an animal or beast due to his distance from tenderness. *"Whoever goes to the doors of the rulers is tested"* means: whoever goes without a dire necessity or need for his going *"is tested"* ("Aftutina"), and this is in the passive form *(sīghat ul-majhūl)* and thus means that the person (who goes to the rulers) falls into *fitna* (a test or predicament). For the person may agree with what the ruler says or does and excuse the ruler and this will be detrimental to the person's *deen*, or the person could oppose what the ruler says or does and this will be detrimental to the person's *dunya*. Al-Madhar said: the hadīth means: whoever sticks to the desert and does not attend the congregational prayer, Jumu'ah, or the gatherings of the *'Ulama* has oppressed himself. As for the one who becomes accustomed to fun and music when hunting then he has become heedless because play and music renders the heart dead. As for the one who hunts for profit then the Sahābah allowed this as they used to hunt. Whoever goes to the rulers and compromises falls into *fitna*, but as for the one who does not compromise and advises the leader with good and forbids them from evil then his entering the (court or palace) of the ruler is better than *jihad*.

Abū Dāwūd related,[1] as did al-Bayhaqī[2] from Abū Hurayrah ﷺ, from the Prophet ﷺ who said:

«قال رسول الله صلى الله عليه وعلى آله وسلم: من بدا جفا، ومن تبع الصيد غفل، ومن أتى أبواب السلطان افتتن، وما ازداد عبد من السلطان دنواً إلاّ ازداد من الله بعداً».

"Whoever lives in the desert[3] becomes harsh, whoever preoccupies himself with following hunting becomes heedless and whoever goes to the doors of the rulers is tested. A slave (of Allāh) does not increase his closeness to the leader except that he increases his distance from Allāh."

---

[1] In *Kitāb us-Sayd* [The Book of Hunting], vol.3, p.111, *hadīth* no.2860, Abū Dāwūd said after relaying the *isnad*: "Meaning the hadīth of Musaddad who said: "whoever sticks to the leader is tested." The remainder of the hadīth is like it."

[2] In the *Sunan*, vol.10, p.101 and his wording was not preceded by anyone and he sufficed with indicating its *isnad* only in *Shu'b ul-Īmān*, vol.7, p.48, no.9404. Imām Ahmad relayed the hadīth in *al-Musnad*, vol.2, p.440.

[3] In the margins of manuscript 'a' it explains what is meant by the word *'badā'* ("to live in the desert"). It refers to living in the desert areas and what is intended is heedlessness as one will jest in regards to matters related to his *deen* and *dunya* in most cases due to placing his trusts on hunting and play. I say: the hadīth of Abū Hurayrah along with what has preceded from Ibn 'Abbās, and along with what will follow in another hadīth from him also, may make it authentic, and with Allāh is success.

Ahmad reported in his *Musnad*,[1] as did al-Bayhaqī[2] with an authentic chain of transmission from Abū Hurayrah ﷺ that: the Messenger of Allāh ﷺ said:

«من بدا جفا، ومن تبع الصيد غفل، ومن أتى أبواب السلطان افتتن، وما ازداد عبد من السلطان قرباً إلا ازداد من الله بعداً».

"Whoever lives in the desert becomes harsh, whoever preoccupies himself with following hunting becomes heedless and whoever goes to the doors of the rulers is tested; a slave (of Allāh) does not increase his closeness to the leader except that he increases his distance from Allāh."[3]

---

[1] Vol.2, p.371

[2] In the *Sunan* in the *hadīth* of Ismā'īl bin Zakariyā' from al-Hasan bin al-Hakam an-Nakha'ī from 'Adiyy bin Thābit from Abū Hāzim from Abū Hurayrah in *Shu'b ul-Īmān*, vol.7, p.47, no.9403.

[3] Also al-Qadā'ī in the *Musnad* of Shihāb, no.339 with the wording *"Whoever lives in the desert becomes harsh, whoever preoccupies himself with following hunting becomes heedless and whoever goes to the doors of the rulers is tested."* Reported by al-Bukhārī in *Kitāb ul-Kunā*, p.70, at-Tabarānī in *al-Mu'jam ul-Kabīr*, no.11030 from the hadīth of Ibn 'Abbās. Ibn 'Adiyy in *al-Kāmil*, vol.1, p.312 via Ismā'īl relayed the hadīth and said: "I do not know anyone who reported the hadīth except Ismā'īl bin Zakariyā and adh-Dhahabī said the same in *al-Mīzān*, vol.1, p.229."

The hadīth is relayed by: Ibn Hibbān, *al-Majrūhīn*, vol.1, p.223, al-'Ajlūnī, *Kashf ul-Khafā'*, vol.2, p.236, Ibn Dayba', *Tamyeez at-Tayyib min al-Khabīth*, p.168, Muhammad Darwish al-Hūt, *Asnā Matālib fī Mukhālifat il-Ahādīth il-Marātib* (Beirut: Dār ul-Kitāb al-'Arabiyyah, 1983 CE), p.286 and Ibn Tāhir al-Hindī, *Tadhkirat ul-Mawdū'āt*, no.768; Shaykh az-Zubaydī said in *It-hāf us-Sādh il-Muttaqīn*, vol.6, p.124: You should know that whenever the "Sultān" is mentioned

Ibn 'Adiyy[1] reports from Abū Hurayrah ﷺ who said: The Messenger of Allāh ﷺ said:

«إن في جهنم وادياً تستعيذ منه كل يوم سبعين مرة، أعده الله للقراء المرائين في أعمالهم وإن أبغض الخلق إلى الله عالم السلطان»

"In Jahannam is a valley which seeks refuge in Allāh seventy times a day which Allāh has prepared for those who recited the Qur'ān just to be seen in their actions.[2] Indeed, the most detested creation to Allāh is the scholar of the sultān."

---

on these chapters the intent with that term is more generally than the Khalīfah and the Amīr. It is anyone who has power, authority and abundant possessions; this is whether he is followed independently or follows another leader.

[1] In *al-Kāmil fi-d-Du'afā*, vol.1, p.468 within the biography of Bakīr bin Shihāb ad-Dāmighānī al-Handhalī with the wording: *"Jahannam seeks refuge from it"* and it also includes "Allāh is preparing it", with the feminine *damīr* instead of the masculine and I think that this is a typo error in the print or mis-spelling *(tas-hīf)*. The end of the hadīth also says: *"...a scholar who visits a Sultān or a worker (for the Sultān)..."*. Ibn 'Adiyy says about the isnad: "Abu'l-Hasan al-Handhalī is majhūl." Ibn Hajar in *at-Taqrīb*, vol.1, 107 says: "Munkar ul-hadīth" and goes to lengths within his biography in *at-Tahdhīb*, vol.1, p.490. Therefore, the hadīth is very weak and Allāh knows best. [TN]: This weak and rejected hadīth is used by the *takfīrīs* of the *'Sayyidoon'* website in an article entitled *"Then know that he is a thief"*, it can be seen here:

http://sayyidoon.wordpress.com/2008/02/08/32then-know-that-he-is-a-thief/

[2] In manuscript 'b' it states "bi A'mālihim" ("with their actions").

Ibn Lāl reports,[1] as does al-Hāfidh Abu'l-Fatayān ad-Dahstānī[2] in *Kitāb Tahdhīr min 'Ulama is-Sū'*, and ar-Rāfi'ī[3] in *Tārīkh Qazwīn* from Abu Hurayrah who said: the Messenger of Allāh ﷺ said:

---

[1] He is Abū Bakr Ahmad bin 'Ali al-Hamadhānī the Imām and Shāfi'ī Faqīh, he was born in 308 AH and heard much (hadīth). He travelled greatly, memorised, he was a polymath *(mutafannin)* and authored a number of classifications in hadīth science even though he was famed in *fiqh*. He also has a *Sunan* and a *Mu'jam us-Sahābah*, an-Nawawī said about him in *at-Tahthīb*: "Lāl: with an alif on the lām and then another lām on the scale of "Māl"." Al-Isnawī said: "Lāl: with two lāms between the alif and it means: *akhras* ('mute'), he died in 398 AH." For his biography see *Tārīkh Baghdād*, vol.4, p.318; *Tabaqāt ul-Isnawī*, vol.2, p.363; *Tahdhīb ul-Asmā'*; an-Nawawī, *al-Lughāt*, vol.2, p.195; adh-Dhahabī, *as-Siyar*, vol.17, p.75; *Shadharāt udh-Dhahab*, vol.3, p.151.

[2] 'Umar bin 'AbdulKarīm bin Sa'dawayh ad-Dahstānī ar-Ra'uwāsī, he was a Hāfidh and heard from al-Khaleelī and as-Sābūnī and compiled and classified, a significant amount of scholars relayed form him such as as-Silafī who gained an *ijāzah* from him. He was a prominent Imām within this field and was born in 428 AH and died in 503 AH. For his biography see *al-'Ibar*, vol.4, p.6; adh-Dhahabī, *Tadhkirat ul-Huffādh*, vol.4, p.1237 and as-Suyūtī, *Tabaqāt ul-Huffādh*, p.451.

[3] He is Abu'l-Qāsim 'AbdulKarīm bin Muhammad ar-Rāfi'ī from the senior Shāfi'ī scholars. He was born in 555 AH and relayed from many, those who relayed from him included al-Mundhirī and others and he was from those *'Ulama* who had *zuhd, wara'* and *taqwā*. Of his works are: *Tārīkh Qazwīn*, *al-Fath ul-Azīz fī Sharh al-Wajīz*, *Sharh Musnad ish-Shāfi'ī* and other works. He died in 623 AH and for his biography see an-Nawawī, *Tahdhīb ul-Asmā'* and *al-Lughāt*, vol.2, p.264; *al-'Ibar*, vol.5, p.94; adh-Dhahabī, *as-Siyar*, vol.22, p.252-255; Ibn Shākir al-Kutabī, *Fawāt*

«إن أبغض الخلق إلى الله تعالى العالم يزور العمال»

"The most hated creation unto Allāh is the scholar who visits the workers (for the ruler)."

In the wording of Abu'l-Fatayān it says:

«إن أهون الخلق على الله: العالم يزور العمال»

"The weakest of creation unto Allāh is: the scholar who visits the workers (for the ruler)."[1]

Ibn Mājah[2] reports from Abū Hurayrah who said: the Messenger of Allāh ﷺ said:

---

ul-Wafayāt, vol.2, pp.7-8; al-Yāfi'ī, *Mirāt ul-Jinān*, vol.4, p.56; Ibn us-Subkī, *Tabaqāt ush-Shāfi'iyyah*, vol.8, pp.281-293; Jamāluddīn Abu'l-Mahāsin Ibn Tughrī Bardī, *an-Nujūm uz-Zāhidah*, vol.6, p.266 and Ibn ul-'Imād, *Shadharāt udh-Dhahab*, vol.5, p.108.

[1] On the margins of manuscript 'a' it is mentioned: This and the likes, which are apparently absolute, depend on if the scholar visits them in regards to their matters with the evidence that it is most likely that he can make the ruler retract from his oppression and to advise him. In this instance this is not prohibited and may even be obligatory and this has to take into consideration the benefits for the creation and not to increase in visiting the ruler.

[2] In the introduction, in the chapter *'Inqitā' bi'l-'Ilm wa'l-'Amal bihi'*, vol.1, pp.93-94, no.255

«إن أبغض القراء إلى الله تعالى الذين يزورون الأمراء»

"The most hated reciters (i.e. or scholars) unto Allāh are those who visit the rulers."[1]

---

[1] In the introduction, *'Bāb Intifā' bi'l-'Ilm wa'l-'Amal bihi'* [Chapter Benefitting from Knowledge and Acting by it], vol.1, p.94, *hadīth* no.256. Tirmidhī transmitted the hadīth in *Kitāb uz-Zuhd*, *'Bāb ma jā fi'r-Riyā' wa's-Sum'a'*, vol.4, pp.593-94, *hadīth* no.2383. Tirmidhī said about the *hadīth*: *hasan gharīb*. Ibn 'Adiyy also transmits the hadīth in *al-Kāmil*, vol.5, p.1727 and says:

> This hadīth was relayed from Bakīr bin Shihāb ad-Dāmighānī from Ibn Sīrīn from Abū Hurayrah and the two narrations do not equalise at all. 'Ammār bin Sayf has other than was has been mentioned and weakness is clear within his hadīth. Ibn ul-Jawzī relayed the hadīth via his own route of transmission and then said: This hadīth is not authentic and Bakīr ad-Dāmighānī is Ibn Shihāb about whom Ibn 'Adiyy said: 'he has rejected ahādīth...'

Al-Albānī said in *al-Mishkāt*, no.275, commenting on the statement of at-Tirmidhī in regards to the hadīth:

> This is what is mentioned in our copy of the Sunan and al-Mundhirī transmitted in *at-Targhīb*, vol.1, p.33 that: 'the hadīth is just gharīb and trying to make it to be a good hadīth is far from being correct, for 'Ammār bin Sayf, who is ad-Dabbī, is weak from Abī Mu'ādh and his name is Sulaymān bin Arqam and he is matrūk (to be left aside), so the hadīth is very weak (da'īf jiddan).' I say: Adh-Dhahabī transmitted some who had deemed 'Ammār bin Sayf to be *thiqah* yet the majority have weakened him. See *al-Mīzān*, vol.3, p.165 and *at-Tahdhīb*, vol.7, pp.402-403. Ibn Hajar said about 'Ammār bin Sayf in *at-Taqrīb*, vol.2, p.47: a weak narrator of hadīth and he was a pious worshipper.

Ad-Daylamī reported in *Musnad ul-Firdaws* from Abu Hurayrah ﷺ who said: the Messenger of Allāh ﷺ said:

«إذا رأيت العالم يخالط السلطان مخالطة كثيرة فاعلم أنه لص»

"If you see a scholar mixing with a ruler often, then know that he is a thief!"[1]

Ibn Mājah reported[2] with a chain of transmission of trustworthy narrators (*thiqāt*)[3] from Ibn 'Abbās ﷺ from the Prophet ﷺ who said:

---

[1] Mentioned in ad-Daylamī, *Firdaws ul-Akhbār*, vol.1, p.276, no.1077 and also in *Kanz ul-'Amāl*, no.28973.

[2] In the introduction, *'Bāb Intifā' bi'l-'Ilm wa'l-'Amal bihi'* [Chapter Benefitting from Knowledge and Acting by it], vol.1, p.93-94, hadīth no.255.

[3] As-Suyūtī's statement "trustworthy narrators" was transmitted from al-Hāfidh al-Mundhirī and this expression is also used often by al-Hāfidh al-Haythamī, yet it does not prove the authenticity of the hadīth as is oft-repeated in *'ilm ul-mustalah il-hadīth* [as a chain of trustworthy narrators may still contain a significant defect, such as a missing link between two of them, etc.]. Al-Hāfidh al-Būsayrī stated in *az-Zawā'id*: "the isnad is weak, for 'Ubaydullāh bin Abī Bardah is unknown." 'Ubaydullāh bin Abī Bardah is also ascribed to his grandfather who was Ibn ul-Mughīrah, Ibn Hajar in *at-Taqrīb*, vol.2, p.539 said that the hadīth is *maqbūl*.

I say: in the *sanad* is al-Walīd bin Muslim who, even though is a trustworthy narrator, made much *tadlīs* as al-Hāfidh said in *at-Taqrīb*, vol.2, p.336. Thus, the hadīth is *da'īf* and al-Albānī deemed it to be weak in *al-Ahādīth ud-Da'īfah*, vol.3, pp.404-405, no.1250, he also some beneficial speech about the *tasāhul* (laxity) of ad-Diyā al-Maqdisī in *al-Mukhtārah* and it is good to refer to it.

«إن ناساً من أمتي سيتفقهون في الدين، ويقرأون القرآن، يقولون نأتي الأمراء، فنصيب من دنياهم، ونعتزلهم بديننا، ولا يكون ذلك! كما لا يجتنى من القتاد إلاّ الشوك، كذلك لا يجتني من قربهم إلاّ ... » قال ابن الصباح: كأنه يعني: الخطايا.

"Indeed a people from my Ummah will acquire understanding of the deen, recite the Qur'ān and say 'we will go to the rulers and partake from their worldly riches and then leave them with our deen (in tact)', but this will not be, just as thorns do not bring forth anything except thorns. Likewise, their closeness to the rulers does not bring anything forth except (Ibn as-Sabāh stated: it is as if he meant) *sin."*

At-Tabarānī reported in *al-Awsat* with a chain of transmission of trustworthy narrators from Thawbān ﷺ, the freed slave of the Messenger of Allāh ﷺ, who asked him: "O Messenger of Allāh! Am I from the Ahl ul-Bayt?" The Messenger of Allāh was silent until Thawbān asked him for a third time and the Messenger of Allāh replied:

«أنت منهم ما لم تقم على باب سدة، أو تأتي أميراً تسأله.»

"Yes, as long as you do not stand at the gate (suddah) of the leader or go to the ruler and ask him (for things)."

Al-Hāfidh al-Mundhirī said in *at-Targhīb wa't-Tarhīb*:[1]

والمراد بالسدة هنا: باب السلطان ونحوه.

The intent of the word *'Suddah'* here is the 'gate of the ruler' and the likes.

At-Tirmidhī reported and he authenticated it,[2] as did an-Nasā'ī, ...[3] and al-Hākim who also authenticated it[4] that: the Messenger of Allāh ﷺ said:

«أنه سيكون بعدي امراء، فمن دخل عليهم فصدقهم بكذبهم، وأعانهم على ظلمهم، فليس منى، ولست منهن، وليس

---

[1] Vol.4, p.244, no.3261.

[2] In *Kitāb ul-Fitan*, no.72, hadīth no.2259, vol.4, pp.525-526.

[3] In *Kitāb ul-Bay'ah*, *'Bāb man lam ya'in Amīran 'alā'dh-Dhulm'* [Chapter: Whoever Does Not Aid a Ruler in Oppression] with the same *sanad* and text, vol.7, pp.160-161.

[TN] these dots are exactly as they are found in the original text and Dr 'Ali Busarīh did not explain this. However, the dots are probably due to either a blank space in the original manuscripts or an illegible piece of writing in the original manuscripts.

[4] Via Mālik bin Maghwal from Abī Hafs from ash-Sha'bī from Ka'b ibn 'Ajrah, with similar wording in at-Tirmidhī, vol.1, p.79.

بوارد على الحوض، ومن لم يدخل عليهم، ولم يعنهم على ظلمهم، ولم يصدقهم بكذبهم، فهو مني، أنا منه، وهو وارد على الحوض»

"There will be after me leaders, whoever enters to visit them, believes them in their lies and helps them in their oppression is not from me and I am not from him, and he will not be admitted into the Hawd. Whoever does not enter to visit them, does not help them in their oppression and does not believe their lies is from me and I am from him and such a person will be admitted into the Hawd."[1]

---

[1] In the *Sunan*, vol.8, p.165 from the hadīth of Sufyān from Abī Hafs from ash-Sha'bī from 'Āsim al-'Adawī from Ka'b ibn 'Ajrah and it has slight additional wordings, also see *Shu'b ul-Īmān*, vol.7, p.46, no.9397. Tirmidhī said "the hadīth is *hasan ghareeb* and I do not know of it except in the hadīth of Mis'ar..."

I say: the 'Āsim who is in the chain is Ibn 'Abdullāh bin 'Āsim bin 'Umar bin al-Khattāb al-'Adawī al-Madanī and al-Hāfidh said in *at-Taqrīb*, vol.1, p.384: "he is da'īf within the fourth level, he died at the beginning of the Abbasid state in 33 AH." The fourth level gained their narrations from the minor successors such as az-Zuhrī and Qatādah as Ibn Hajar states in the introduction to his book *al-Ānif udh-Dhikr*, vol.1, p.5, and it is also not mentioned that 'Āsim narrated from Ka'b ibn 'Ajrah as it is doubtful that he even meet him let alone narrated from him as Ka'b died after 50 AH while he was about 70 years of age as mentioned by al-Hāfidh Ibn Hajar in *at-Taqrīb*, vol.2, p.135. So the chain is *munqati'* (broken) and additionally 'Āsim is a weak narrator. Refer to his biography in *al-Kāmil*, vol.5, pp.1866-1869; adh-Dhahabī, *al-Mīzān*, vol.2, pp.353-354; Ibn Hajar, *at-Tahdhīb*, vol.5, pp.46-49. In the other chain of transmission used by al-Hākim bin Maghwal from both Sufyān and Mis'ar, 'Āsim al-'Adawī is dropped from the chain and Ibrāhīm ibn Yazīd bin

Ahmad reported,[1] as did Abū Ya'lā[2] and also Ibn Hibbān in his *Sahīh*[1] from Abū Sa'īd al-Khudrī ﷺ from the Prophet ﷺ who said:

Shareek at-Taymī Abū Asmā al-Kūfī is placed in the chain yet this does not prove anything as Ibrāhīm is *mudallis* as Ibn Hajar clarified in *at-Tahdhīb*, vol.1, p.177 and in *at-Taqrīb*, vol.1, pp.45-46. Ibrāhīm also narrated from 'Ā'ishah and Hafsah yet was not around during their time as ad-Dāraqutnī highlighted in al-Hāfidh al-'Ulāi'ī, *Jāmi' ut-Tahsīl*, p.176 and Ibn Hajar, *at-Tahdhīb*, vol.1, p.177. It is doubtful that Ibrahīm heard from Ka'b as Ibrāhīm died in 92 AH as mentioned in *at-Taqrīb*, vol.1, p.46, while 'Ā'ishah ﷺ died in 57 AH as mentioned in *at-Taqrīb*, vol.2, p.606. Therefore, as mentioned previously the *hadīth* in this route is a broken *hadīth* (*munqati'*).

[1] In his *Musnad*, vol.3, pp.24-92 via two routes of transmission:

The first via the hadīth of Yahyā from Shu'bah from Qatādah from Sulaymān bin Abū Sulaymān from Abū Sa'īd al-Khudrī.

The second via the hadīth of Muhammad bin Ja'far from Shu'bah from Qatādah from Sulaymān, or Abū Sulaymān.

From the hadīth of Hajjāj who said: Shu'bah narrated to me: a man from the Quraysh said, from Abū Sa'īd al-Khudrī.

[2] In his *Musnad*, vol.2, pp.404-405, hadīth no.1187 and also vol.2, p.465, hadīth no.1286, the commentator of an edition of this *Musnad*, Professor Husayn Asad stated:

> The *isnad* is *hasan* (good), Sulaymān ibn Abī Sulaymān was mentioned by Ibn Abī Hātim with neither a *jarh* nor a *ta'dīl*. He was also mentioned by Ibn Hibbān as being from the *thiqāt* of the tābi'īn and Ibn Hibbān also said: 'he narrated from Abī Hurayrah and Abī Sa'īd and al-'Awwām bin Hawshab and Qatādah transmitted from him'...

«تكون أمراء تغشاهم غواش وحواش من الناس»

"There will be leaders who will be overwhelmed by cheats and insignificant people."

Ahmad reported, ...,[2] as did al-Bazzār[3] and Ibn Hibbān in his *Sahīh*[1] from Jābir bin 'Abdillāh ﷺ that the Messenger of Allāh ﷺ said:

---

[1] *Mawārid udh-Dhamān*, p.379, hadīth no.1575. I say: al-Haythamī says in *al-Majma'*, vol.5, pp.249-250: 'Reported by Ahmad and Abū Ya'la with the addition of: "we are free from him and he is free from us" and within the *isnad* is Sulaymān ibn Abī Sulaymān al-Qurashī and I do not know of him but the rest of the narrators in the isnad are men of authenticity.' Sulaymān ibn Abī Sulaymān al-Hāshimī is the freed-slave of Ibn 'Abbās as mentioned by Ibn Hajar in *at-Tahdhīb*, vol4, pp.196-197. Al-Bukhārī stated in *at-Tārīkh*: 'Sulaymān ibn Abī Sulaymān from Abī Sa'eed, and from Qatādah, does not mention if he heard from Abī Sa'eed.' Ibn Hajar stated: 'ad-Dāraqutnī stated in *al-'Ilal*: he is majhūl and only Qatādah narrated from him.' Al-Hāfidh al-Būsayrī stated in *Mukhtasar Ithāf al-Maharah*, vol.2, p.206: the hadīth has other supporting narrations from the hadīth of Ibn 'Umar in the *Musnad* of Ahmad bin Manī'; from the hadīth of Khabbāb bin al-Arat as reported by Abū Ya'la al-Mawsilī, at-Tabarānī and Ibn Hibbān in his *Sahīh*; and from the hadīth of an-Nu'mān bin Bashīr reported by Abū Ya'lā al-Mawsilī and Ahmad bin Hanbal...
I say: the *hadīth* is *sahīh* with its routes and other supporting narrations.

[2] In the *Musnad*, vol.3, pp.321-399.
[TN] these dots are exactly as they are found in the original text and Dr 'Ali Busarīh did not explain this. However, the dots are probably due to either a blank space in the original manuscripts or an illegible piece of writing in the original manuscripts.

[3] In al-Haythamī, *Kashf ul-Astār*, hadīth no.1609

«ستكون أمراء من دخل عليهم فأعانهم على ظلمهم،
وصدقهم بكذبهم، فليس مني، ولست منه، ولن يرد على
الحوض، ومن لم يدخل عليهم، ولم يعنهم على ظلمهم، ولم يصدقهم
بكذبهم، فهو مني وأنا منه وسيرد على الحوض».

"There will be rulers after me, and whoever visits them, helps them on their oppression and believes their lies is not from me and I am not from him and he will not be admitted into the Hawd. Whoever does not enter to visit them, does not help them in their oppression and does not believe their lies is from me and I am from him and such a person will be admitted into the Hawd."

Ash-Shīrāzī[2] reported in *al-Alqāb* from Ibn 'Umar ﷺ who said: The Messenger of Allāh ﷺ said:

---

[1] In *Mawārid udh-Dhamān* with the same route of transmission as Ahmad, al-Haythamī said in *al-Majma'*, vol.8, p.250: reported by Ahmad and al-Bazzār and both of their men are men of authenticity.

[2] He is Imām al-Hāfidh Abū Bakr Ahmad bin 'AbdurRahmān ash-Shīrāzī and he heard from al-Qutay'ī, at-Tabarānī, al-Ismā'īlī, Abā'sh-Shaykh, Ibn 'Adiyy and others. Those who narrated from him were: Muhammad bin 'Īsā, Abū Muslim bin Ghazu, Humayd bin al-Ma'mūn, Abu'l-Farj al-Bajlī and al-Khalīlī in turn narrated from them. Al-Khalīlī used to say "Ahmad bin Abī Muslim al-Fārisī al-Hāfidh narrated to us", al-Mustaghfirī said: "he used to understand and memorise." Ad-

«إنها ستكون أمراء، فمن صدقهم بكذبهم، وأعانهم على ظلمهم، وغشي أبوابهم، فليس مني ولست منه، ولا يرد علي الحوض، ومن لم يصدقهم بكذبهم، ولم يعنهم على ظلمهم ولم يغش أبوابهم، فهو مني وسيرد علي الحوض»

"Indeed there will be rulers after me, whoever believes their lies and helps them in their oppression and frequents their gates is not from me and I am not from him and he will not be admitted into the Hawd. Whoever neither believes their lies nor helps them in their oppression, and does not frequent their gates, is from me and will be admitted into the Hawd."

Daylamī said about ash-Shīrāzī: 'he was *thiqah, sādiq*, a *hāfidh* and perfected this field well.' Adh-Dhahabī stated: 'he was of the knights of hadīth and travelled far and wide.' Of his works are: *al-Alqāb* and it is still in manuscript form, he died in Shawwāl in 407 AH. For his biography refer to: Yāqūt al-Hamawī, *Mu'jam ul-Buldān*, vol.3, p.281; adh-Dhahabī, *Tadhkirat ul-Huffādh*, vol.3, pp.1065-1068, *Siyar A'lām un-Nubalā'*, vol.7, pp.242-243 and *al-'Ibar*, vol.3, p.93; as-Safadī, *al-Wāfī bi'l-Wafayāt*, vol.7, p.38; al-Yāfi'ī, *Marāt ul-Janān*, vol.3, p.20; as-Suyūtī, *Tabaqāt ul-Huffādh*, pp.415-416; Hājī Khalīfah, *Kashf udh-Dhunūn*, vol.1, p.157; Ibn ul-'Imād, *Shadharāt udh-Dhahab*, vol.3, pp.184-190; *Hadiyat ul-'Ārifīn*, vol.1, p.71.

Al-Hasan bin Sufyān[1] reported in his *Musnad*,[2] as did al-Hākim in *at-Tārīkh*,[3] Abū Nu'aym,[4] al-'Uqaylī,[1] ad-Daylamī[2] and ar-Rāfi'ī in his *Tārīkh*,[3] from Anas bin Mālik ﷺ who said; The Messenger of Allāh ﷺ said:

---

[1] He is Imām al-Hāfidh Abu'l-'Abbās al-Hasan bin Sufyān bin 'Āmir ash-Shaybānī al-Khurasānī, author of *al-Musnad*. He was born in the year 283 AH and travelled to the horizons to hear from Ahmad bin Hanbal, Qutaybah bin Sa'eed, Shaybān bin Farrūkh and many others. Ibn Khuzaymah, Muhammad bin Ya'qūb bin il-Akhram, Abū 'Ali al-Hāfidh, al-Ismā'eelī, Ibn Hibbān and many others. Al-Hākim said:

> Al-Hasan bin Sufyān was the Muhaddith of Khurasān of his time and was ahead in verification, abundance, *fahm* (understanding), *fiqh* (comprehension) and *adab* (manners). He ﷺ died in the year 303 AH in the village Bālūz which is three farāsikh (9 miles) from the city of Nasā.

His biography can be found in: Ibn Abī Hātim, *al-Jarh wa't-Ta'dīl*, vol.3, p.16, Ibn ul-Jawzī, *al-Muntadham*, vol.6, pp.132-136, Adh-Dhahabī, *Tadhkirat ul-Huffādh*, vol.2, pp.703-705, Adh-Dhahabī, *Mīzān ul-'I'tidāl*, vol.1, pp.492-493, Adh-Dhahabī, *as-Siyar*, vol.14, p.157, Ibn Hajar, *Lisān ul-'Arab*, vol.2, p.211 and Ibn ul-'Imād, *Shadharāt udh-Dhahab*, vol.2, p.241.

[2] The author (as-Suyūtī) ascribes it to him (al-Hasan bin Sufyān) in *al-Lālī' ul-Masnū'ah fi'l-Ahādīth il-Mawdū'ah*, vol.1, p.219 from the hadīth of Mukhallad bin Mālik from Ibrāhīm bin Rustum.

[3] The author (as-Suyūtī) ascribes it to him (al-Hākim) in *al-Lālī' ul-Masnū'ah fi'l-Ahādīth il-Mawdū'ah*, vol.1, p.219 with his wording from the hadīth of Muhammad bin Ya'qūb: Muhammad bin al-Hajjāj bin 'Īsā narrated to us: Ibrāhīm bin Rustum narrated to us: 'Umar Abū Hafs al-'Abdī from Ismā'īl bin Samī' from Anas in a *marfū'* form.

[4] I found it in a *mawqūf* form from Ja'far bin Muhammad as-Sādiq and he is as what the author mentions about him himself in *al-Hilyah*, vol.3, p.194.

[1] I neither found the hadīth in *ad-Du'afā ul-Kabīr* by al-'Uqaylī nor in *al-Fahāris ul-'Alamiyyah*, also I did not find it within the biographies of those mentioned in the *sanad* of the hadīth. I did however find it, by the *tawfīq* of Allāh, with Ibn 'AbdulBarr in *Jāmi' Bayān ul-'Ilm wa Fadlihi*, vol.1, p.227 wherein he said:

> Abū Ja'far al-'Uqaylī mentioned it saying: 'Abdullāh bin Muhammad bin Sa'dawayh al-Marwazī informed us: 'Alī bin Hasan al-Marwazī narrated to us: Ibrāhīm bin Rustum narrated to us: Hafs al-Abrī narrated to us: from Ismā'eel bin Samī' from Anas who said: "The Messenger of Allāh ﷺ said..." and then he mentioned the hadīth.

Abū Ja'far said: the hadīth of this Hafs are unreliable (ghayru mahfūdh). I say: I mainly think that there has occurred an error in the printed copy that we have and also the *sanad* mentioned here is different from that mentioned prior by al-Hākim and al-Hasan bin Sufyān. Hafs al-Abrī and Allāh knows best if this is either a *tas-hīf* (textual error) by 'Umar Abī Hafs al-'Abdī or of Hafs al-Ablī as will be mentioned later. Because the copy of the printed edition of *al-Jāmi'* has typo errors and textual errors *(tas-hīfāt)* and thus it needs to be re-published, re-distributed and academically checked and edited. My Allāh aid a researcher to do this.

[2] The author (as-Suyūtī) ascribes it to him (ad-Daylamī) in *al-La'ālī' ul-Masnū'ah fi'l-Ahādīth il-Mawdū'ah*, vol.1, p.220 and transmits it with the *isnād*.

[TN]: as-Suyūtī, *al-La'ālī' ul-Masnū'ah fi'l-Ahādīth il-Mawdū'ah* (Bayrūt, Dār al-Ma'rifah lil-Ṭiba'ah wa'an-Nashr, 1975, 1st Edn./1983, 2nd Edn.)

[3] I say: al-'Allāmah ash-Shawkānī said in *al-Fawā'id ul-Majmū'ah*, pp.288-289:

> The *'Ulama* are those who have been entrusted by the Messengers" – it is *mawdū'ah* (fabricated) and within the *isnad* is one who is *majhūl* and one who is *matrūk*.

Al-'Allāmah, al-Muhaddith, al-Muhaqqiq al-Mu'allimī al-Yamānī commented on this saying:

> Ibn ul-Jawzī mentioned it (vol.1, p.263) via Ibrāhīm bin Rustum from 'Umar Abū Hafs al-'Abdī from Ismā'īl bin Samī' from Anas in *marfū'* form. Muhammad bin Mu'āwiyah followed from Muhammad bin Yazīd from Ismā'īl and al-'Abdī is *matrūk*, as for Ibrāhīm then he is *majhūl* (unknown) and Muhammad bin Mu'āwiyah is a *kadhdhāb* (liar).

I say: as-Suyūtī mentioned it has been relayed with this wording from the hadīth of 'Ali bin Abī Tālib in a *marfū'* form reported by al-'Askarī. It was also relayed in *marfū'* form up to Ja'far bin Muhammad and reported by Abū Nu'aym in *al-Hilyah* and it has a supporting narration in the hadīth of 'Umar bin al-Khattāb that has been reported by ad-Daylamī in *Musnad ul-Firdaws*. There are many other authentic and *hasan* supporting narrations with the same meaning which number over 40 narrations. Al-Yamānī said in his commentary and claims:

> Al-'Abdī is not *matrūk* rather he is of the men (narrators) of the *Sunan* and Ahmad and others deemed him to be *thiqah* (trustworthy). 'AbdusSamad said: 'he is above *thiqah*.'

I say: as-Suyūtī was confused and held that 'Umar bin Hafs (Bin Dhakwān) who was in the *sanad* was Abū Hafs al-'Abdī, a biography of him is found in *al-Lisān*, vol.4, p.298, no.832. Imām Ahmad said: "We have left off his hadīth and we burn them (his hadīth papers)!" He just had a few *ahādīth*, when he arrived in Baghdād the people gathered around him and he began to narrate that which was not from his hadīth. As for the one who Imām Ahmad considered *thiqah*, and the one about which 'AbdusSamad said "he is above thiqah", then that is Abū Hafs 'Umar bin Ibrāhīm al-'Abdī, a biography of him is found in *at-Tahdhīb*, vol.7, p.425, no.694. this clarifies that 'Umar Abū Hafs mentioned in the *sanad* is well-known by his *kunyah* and 'Umar bin Hafs was well known for his *kunyah*. Both men have biographies in *al-Mīzān* and in the section on *kunyahs* only Ibn Hafs is mentioned. Ibn Ibrāhīm has a biography in *at-Tahdhīb* yet his *kunyah* is not mentioned in the chapter on *kunyahs*. Shaykh al-Albānī mentioned him in *Da'īf ul-Jāmi' as-Saghīr*,

«العلماء أمناء الرسل على عباد الله ما لم يخالطوا السلطان فإذا فعلوا ذلك فقد خانوا الرسل فاحذروهم واعتزلوهم»

"The 'Ulama are those who have been entrusted by the Messengers over the servants of Allāh as long as they do not mix with the ruler, if they do that then they have betrayed the Messengers so be warned of them and stay away from them."[1]

Al-'Askarī reports from 'Ali bin Abī Tālib ﷺ who said: The Messenger of Allāh ﷺ said:

«الفقهاء أمناء الرسل ما لم يدخلوا في الدنيا ويتبعوا السلطان، فإذا فعلوا ذلك فاحذروهم»

"The Fuqahā are those who have been entrusted by the Messengers as long as they do not become engulfed in the dunya and follow the ruler, if they do this then be warned of them."[2]

---

p.566, no.3883 (2nd Edn., 1988) and ascribed it to al-Hasan bin Sufyān and al-Bayhaqī saying "da'īf".

[1] [TN] This narration is mentioned in the books of the *mawdū'āt* (fabricated ahādīth) and the chain contains Ibrāhīm ibn Rustum who is *majhūl* (unknown) yet Yahyā ibn Ma'īn and others considered him to be trustworthy.

[2] The author (as-Suyūtī) ascribes the hadīth to him in *al-La'āli' ul-Masnū'ah fi'l-Ahādīth il-Mawdū'ah*, vol.1, p.220 and so does al-Hāfidh as-Sakhāwī in *al-Maqāsid*

Al-Hākim reported in his *at-Tārīkh*,[1] and so did ad-Daylamī,[2] from Mu'ādh ibn Jabal ﷺ who said: The Messenger of Allāh ﷺ said:

«ما من عالم أتى صاحب سلطان طوعاً إلا كان شريكه في كل لون يعذب به في نار جهنم»

---

al-Hasanah, no.746 from the hadīth of al-'Awwām bin Hawshab from Abū Sādiq from 'Alī in *marfū* form. Imām as-Sakhāwī said: "the sanad is da'īf" and likewise is found in *Tamyīz ut-Tayyib min al-Khabīth* by Ibn ud-Dayba', p.114. Az-Zurqānī said in *Mukhtasar ul-Maqāsid*, no.693: "da'īf". It is also in *Kashf ul-Khafā'* by al-'Ajlūnī, vol.2, p.271 and Shaykh al-Albānī said: "da'īf" as is found in *Da'īf ul-Jāmi'*, p.587, no.4032.

[TN] 'AbdurRahmān bin 'Alī ibn ud-Dayba', *Tamyīz ut-Tayyib min al-Khabīth fimāyuduru 'ala'l-Alsinat in-Nās min il-Hadīth* (Beirut: Dār Kitāb al-'Arabī, 1970 CE). It was also published in Egypt in 1324 AH (1906 CE) and by Maktabat wa-Matba'at Muhammad 'Ali Sabih, 1963 also in Egypt. The author Ibn Dayba' is: 'AbdurRahmān bin 'Alī bin Muhammad bin 'Umar ash-Shaybānī ash-Shāfi'ī al-Atharī (1461-1537 CE). He also authored: *Mukaffirat adh-Dhunub wa-Mujibat al-Jannah* (Cairo: Dār ul-I'tisam, 1976, 2nd Edn.); *Taysir al-Wusūl ila Jāmi' al-Usūl*, Egypt: Mustafa al-Babi al-Halabi,1934 CE, 1st Edn. ;1968-69, 2nd Edn.; Beirut: Dar al-Ma'rifah, 1977.

[1] Al-Hāfidh as-Sakhāwī ascribes it to him in *al-Maqāsid*, no.983 and said "it is not authentic" and this is also mentioned by Ibn ad-Dayba' in *at-Tamyīz*, p.149. it is also in *Kashf ul-Khafā'* by al-'Ajlūnī and by Ibn Tāhir al-Fatanī in *Tadhkirat ul-Mawdū'āt*, p.25. Al-Albānī said: "da'īf" as is found in *Da'īf ul-Jāmi'*, p.750, no.5193.

[2] Ibid.

"There is no scholar who goes to the one who has authority out of obedience except that he has become a partner in everything that he will be punished for in the Hellfire."

Abu'sh-Shaykh reported in *ath-Thawāb* from Mu'ādh ibn Jabal ﷺ who said: The Messenger of Allāh ﷺ said:

«إذا قرأ الرجل القرآن وتفقه في الدين، ثم أتى باب السلطان تملقا إليه وطمعا لما في يده خاض بقدر خطاه في نار جهنم»

"If a man reads the Qur'ān, understands the deen and then goes to the gate of the ruler flattering him and aspiring for what the ruler has in his hand will be thrown into Hellfire depending upon the extent of his sin."[1]

Ad-Daylamī reported from Ibn 'Abbās ﷺ who said: The Messenger of Allāh ﷺ said:

---

[1] Al-Albānī ascribed the hadīth to him (Abu'sh-Shaykh) in *Da'īf ul-Jāmi'* by Abu'sh-Shaykh and ad-Daylamī in *al-Firdaws* and said: "da'īf". See *Da'īf ul-Jāmi'*, p.90, no.629.

«سيكون في آخر الزمان علماء يرغبون الناس يرغبون الناس في الآخرة ولا يرغبون ويزهدون الناس في الدنيا ولا يزهدون، وينهون عن غشيان الأمراء ولا ينتهون»

"There will be at the end of time 'Ulama who motivate the people about the Hereafter but do not encourage themselves and tell the people to be ascetic in the dunya but are not ascetic themselves, and forbid from going to the rulers but do not forbid themselves."[1]

Ad-Daylamī reported from 'Umar ibn al-Khattāb ﷺ who said: The Messenger of Allāh ﷺ said:

«إن الله يحب الأمراء إذا خالطوا العلماء، ويمقت العلماء إذا خالطوا الأمراء، لأن العلماء إذا خالطوا الأمراء رغبوا في الدنيا، والأمراء إذا خالطوا العلماء رغبوا في الآخرة».

"Allāh loves the rulers who mix with the 'Ulama and hates the 'Ulama who mix with the rulers, because if the 'Ulama mix with

[1] The like is found in *al-Firdaws*, vol.2, p.314, no.3422.

[TN] Nūh ibn Abī Maryam is in the chain and he is famous for lying.

the rulers they will encouraged towards the dunya and if the rulers mix with the 'Ulama they will be encouraged to the Hereafter."[1]

Abū 'Amr ad-Dānī[2] reported in the book *al-Fitan* from al-Hasan who said: The Messenger of Allāh ﷺ said:

«لا تزال الأمة تحت يد الله وكنفه، ما لم يمار قراؤها أمراءها»

"This Ummah will not cease to be under the Hand of Allāh as long as its reciters (i.e. scholars) do not argue with its leaders."[1]

---

[1] [TN] According to the edition by Muhaqqiq Majdi as-Sayyid, this hadīth is da'īf.

[2] His name is: 'Uthmān bin Sa'eed al-Andalūsī al-Qurtubī and then "ad-Dānī". He was born in the year 371 and was an Imām in hadīth and the Qur'anic sciences. He travelled to heard from many and authored *tasānīf* (classifications) particularly in regards to the *qira'āt*. He died in the year 444 AH (CE) ﷺ. For his biography refer to: Al-Humaydī, *Jadhwat ul-Muqtabis*, p.305, Ibn Bashkuwāl, *as-Silah*, vol.2, pp.405-407 and Ad-Dabbī, *Bughyat ul-Multamis*, pp.411-412.

[TN] Abu'l-Qāsim Khalaf bin 'AbdulMālik Ibn Bashkuwāl ("the son of Pascual"), (494–587 AH/1101-1183 CE), was a scholar who had spent most of his life in Cordoba but also lived in Seville. His book *Kitāb as-Silah: fī tārīkh a'immat al-Andalus wa-'Ulamā'ihim wa-Muhaddithīhim wa-Fuqahāihim wa-Udabāihim* was printed in Cairo in 1374 AH/1955 CE and in 1994 edited by 'Izzat al-'Attar al-Husaynī. *Kitāb us-Silah* is a supplement to al-Faradī's work *Tārīkh 'Ulama ul-Andalus.* He is said to have authored over fifty works but only two of these are remaining, *Kitāb us-Silah* being one of them. Ad-Dabbī's (d. 599/1203) *Bughyat ul-Multamis fi't-Tārīkh Rijāl il-Andalus* was printed in Madrid in 1885 CE by Bibliotheca Arabico-Hispana and edited by F. Codera and J. Ribera.

Al-Hākim reports and authenticates from 'Abdullāh bin ash-Shukhiyyir ﷺ[2] who said: The Messenger of Allāh ﷺ said:

«أقلوا الدخول على الأغنيا، فإنه أجدر ألا تزدروا نعمة الله»

"Lessen your visits to the rich this will ensure that you do not disdain Allāh's favours."[3]

---

[1] It is also in *al-Majma'*, no.1105, folio 37/'b' in a *mursal* form and within the *isnad* is Khulayd bin Hassān about whom as-Salmānī said: "there are some issues with him". Ibn Hibbān mentioned him in *ath-Thiqāt* and said "he makes mistakes and gets confused". Al-Khalīlī mentioned him in *al-Irshād* and said "there is no agreement on him rather he writes hadīth for consideration...". Also see Ibn Hajar, *al-Lisān*, vol.2, p.496. al-Hāfidh al-'Irāqī in *Takhrīj Ahādīth ul-Ihyā'*, vol.2, p.150 after ascribing it to Abī 'Amru ad-Dānī in *al-Fitan* from the *mursal* narration of al-Hasan, "its isnad is weak".

[2] With a *kasra* on the *shīn* and a *shaddah* on the *khā*, he is: Ibn 'Awf al-'Āmirī, for his biography refer to: *Tabaqāt Ibn Sa'd*, vol.4, p.311; Ibn Hajar, *at-Tahdhīb*, vol.5, p.251; Ibn Hajar, *at-Taqrīb*, vol.1, p.422; Ibn Hajar, *al-Isābah*, vol.2, p.324.

[3] In *al-Mustadrak*, vol.4, p.312, al-Hākim said: "Sahīh isnad" and adh-Dhahabī agreed with him and left its *isnād* in the original print and thus was unable to make a ruling on it. Then I found the hadīth in al-'Uqaylī in *ad-Du'afā'*, vol.3, p.327 in the biography of 'Ammār bin Zarabī. Al-'Uqaylī said: "He ('Ammār bin Zarabī) is a Basrī and was mainly confused in his hadīth. Of his hadīth are what Hajjāj bin 'Amrān as-Sadūsī narrated o us who said: 'Ammār bin Zarabī narrated to us saying: Bishr bin Mansūr narrated to us: from Shu'ayb bin al-Habhāb from Abi'l-'Āliyah from Mutarraf from his father..." From the hadīth of al-Hasan bin Sufyān it has the same *sanad* and *matn* reported by Ibn 'Adiyy in *al-Kāmil*, vol.5, p.1731. Ibn 'Adiyy

Al-Hakīm at-Tirmidhī[1] reported in *Nawādir ul-Usūl* from 'Umar bin al-Khattāb ﷺ who said: The Messenger of Allāh ﷺ came to me and I knew that there was grief in his face, he took me by my beard and said:

---

states: "This hadīth with this isnād is unreliable (*ghayru mahfūdh*)." Adh-Dhahabī stated in *al-Mīzān*, vol.3, p.164 after transmitting the hadīth of 'Ammār bin Zarabī and what al-'Uqaylī said about him: "He heard from 'Ammār bin Zarabī 'Abdān al-Ahwazī and then left of him and accused him of lying and al-Hasan bin Sufyān and Abū Ya'lā." Ibn Hajar stated in *al-Lisān*, vol.4, p.312: "Ibn Abī Hātim said: I asked an-Nabātī about him and he said 'he is a liar, his hadīth are abandoned' and criticised his hadīth and did not read them to us." Ibn Hibbān said in *ath-Thiqāt*: "he was the Imām of Masjid 'Amru ibn Marzūq, he was blind and used to relay strange hadīth and err." Shaykh, al-Muhaqqiq al-Albānī said in *Da'īf ul-Jāmi'*, p.152, no.1080: "da'īf".

[1] [TN] Abū 'Abdullāh Muhammad ibn 'Ali al-Hakīm at-Tirmidhī was born in Tirmidh ("Termez" in southern Uzbekistan near the border with Afghanistan) in 820 CE and died between 905 and 910 CE (293-298 AH), he is celebrated by the Sūfīs. There are a number of works that are attributed to him, a few of which have been edited and published but many of which are still within manuscript form within various libraries in Paris and Istanbul: *Nawādir ul-Usūl* [The Rarities of the Principles], *Bayān al-Farq Bayna's-Sadr wa'l-Qalb wa'l-Fu'ād wa'l-Lub* [An Exposition of the Difference between the Chest, Heart and Inner Core] (translated into English by Nicholas Heer); *Kitāb ul-'Ilal*; *al-Masā'il al-Maknūnah*; *al-Furūq wa man' at-Taraduf* (Cairo: an-Nahar, 1998, ed. Muhammad Ibrahīm al-Juyūshi); *Bad' ush-Sha'n; Kitāb Bayān ul-'Ilm; Jawāb Kitāb min ar-Rayy, Jawāb ul-Masā'il alati sa'aluhu Ahl is-Sarakhs* [Answering Questions Posed by the People of Sarakhs], *Kitāb Daqā'iq ul-'Ulūm; Sirāt ul-Awliya* and *Khatm ul-Awliya.*

« إِنَّا لِلَّهِ وَإِنَّا إِلَيهِ رَاجِعون أتاني جبريل آنفاً، فقال لي: إن أمتك مفتتنه بعدك بقليل من الدهر، غير كثير، قلت: ومن أين ذلك ! ؟ قال: من قبل قرائهم وأمرائهم، يمنع الأمراء الناس حقوقهم، فلا يعطونها، وتتبع القراء أهواء الأمراء قلت: يا جبريل ! فبم يسلم من يسلم منهم ؟

Adh-Dhahabī in his *Tadhkirat al-Huffādh* relates on the authority of as-Sulamī, a famous fourth century historian and biographer, that Hakīm al-Tirmidhī was banished from Tirmidh because of his having written two books: *Khatm al-Awliyā'* and *Kitāb al-'Ilal.* The specialist of the works and ideas of Hakīm at-Tirmidhī in Europe is the German academic Bernd Radtke who has produced tens of works, translations and studies of the works and beliefs of al-Hakīm at-Tirmidhī. One of Radtke's better known works in this regard is *The Concept of Sainthood in Early Islamic Mysticism: Two Works by Al-Hakim Al-Tirmidhi*, trans. Bernd Radtke and John O'Kane (Surrey, UK: Curzon Press, 1996). Of the odd Sufic stories connected to al-Hakīm at-Tirmidhī is what is mentioned in an article by Camille Adams Helminski entitled *Women and Sufism* in the journal *Gnosis*, no.30, Winter 1994. Helminski states:

> The wife of the ninth-century Sufi Al-Hakim at-Tirmidhi was a mystic in her own right. She used to dream for her husband as well as for herself. Khidr, the mysterious one, would appear to her in her dreams. One night he told her to tell her husband to guard the purity of his house.

قال: بالكف والصبر، إن أعطوا الذي لهم أخذوه وإن منعوه تركوه».

"From Allāh we came and unto Him we shall return! Jibrīl came to me earlier and said to me: 'Your Ummah will shortly be tried after you and it won't be long before this happens.' I said: 'Where will this come from?' He said: 'Due to their reciters and rulers, for the rulers will not give people their rights while the reciters will follow the desires of the rulers.' I said: 'O Jibrīl, with what will one be saved?' He said, 'By holding back and patience, so if they are given what is their (right) they take it and if they are prevented from it (their right) they leave it.'

Al-Hākim reported from 'Abdullāh bin al-Hārith ﷺ[1] that he heard the Prophet ﷺ say:

---

[1] He is 'Abdullāh bin al-Hārith bin Jaza', the knowledgeable companion who lived long, he narrated a number of hadīth and relayed from the Imāms. He witnessed the conquest of Egypt and its inhabitants, he was the last companion to die as he lived long and became blind, he died in 87 AH according to the most correct dating. There are biographies of him in: *Tabaqāt Ibn Sa'd*, vol.4, p.497; *Tabaqāt Khalīfah*, no.495 and 2715; Yāqūb al-Fasawī, *al-Ma'rifah wa't-Tārīkh*, vol.1, p.268; *al-Jarh wa't-Ta'dīl*, vol.30, p.5; *al-Mustadrak*, vol.3, p.633; *al-Hilyah*, vol.2, p.6; Ibn 'AbdulBarr, *al-Istī'āb*, p.883; Ibn ul-Athīr, *Asad ul-Ghābah*, vol.3, p.203; adh-

«سيكون بعدي سلاطين، الفتن على أبوابهم كمبارك الإبل، لا يعطون أحداً شيئاً، إلا أخذوا من دينه مثله» .

"There will be rulers after me and tribulation is at their doors just like the kneeling places of the camels. They do not give anyone anything except that they will take the like from his deen."[1]

Ad-Daylamī reported from Abi'l-A'war as-Sulamī ﷺ[2] that he said:

Dhahabī, *al-'Ibar*, vol.1, p.101; adh-Dhahabī, *as-Siyar*, vol.3, p.387; *Marāt ul-Janān*, vol.1, p.177; Ibn Hajar, *al-Isābah fī Tamyīz is-Sahābah*, vol.2, p.291; Ibn Hajar, *Tahdhīb ut-Tahdhīb*, vol.5, p.178; as-Suyūtī, *Husn ul-Muhādharah*, vol.1, p.212; Ibn ul-'Imād, *Shadharāt udh-Dhahab*, vol.1, p.97

[1] In *al-Mustadrak*, vol.3, p.634 via Hassān bin Ghālib from Ibn Lahī'ah from Abū Zur'ah 'Amru bin Jābir from 'Abdillāh bin al-Hārith bin Jaza' ﷺ. I say: both al-Hākim and adh-Dhahabī were silent about this hadīth. In the *sanad* is 'Amru bin Jābir and he is *da'īf*, see adh-Dhahabī, *al-Mīzān*, vol.3, p.250; Ibn Hajar, *at-Tahdhīb*, vol.8, p.11 and Ibn Hajar, *at-Taqrīb*, vol.2, p.66. also in the *sanad* is Hassān bin Ghālib, adh-Dhahabī said: "He is *matrūk* as Ibn Hibbān mentioned, he is a Shaykh from the people of Egypt who used to confuse narrations and narrate from... .it is not allowed to narrate from him except via consideration...." Al-Hākim said: "He has narrated fabricated hadīth (allegedly) from Mālik." See *Al-Mīzān*, vol.1, p.479-480 and Ibn Hajar, *al-Lisān*, vol.1, p.238. al-Hāfidh al-Haythamī said: *"at-Tabarānī reports the hadīth and within it is Hassān bin Ghālib and he is matrūk."* See *Majma' uz-Zawā'id*, vol.5, p.249. Shaykh al-Albānī said about the hadīth: "very weak" as is found in *Da'īf ul-Jāmi'*, p.485, no.3306.

[2] He is 'Amru bin Sufyān, the companion, he died in 65 AH. Refer to Ibn Hajar, *al-Isābah*, vol.2, pp.540-541, no.5851.

"Beware of the doors of the ruler!"[1]

Al-Hasan bin Sufyān reported in his *Musnad*, and so did ad-Daylamī,[2] from Ibn 'Umar ﷻ who said: the Messenger of Allāh ﷺ said:

[TN] he was one of the generals of Mu'āwiyah ﷻ. This hadīth was been mentioned in an article entitled *'Let the Scholars Beware'* by some of the cult followers of Omar Bakri Muhammad Fustuq al-Mudallis. However, they mention "Abu'l-A'war as-Silmī" getting the name of the companion incorrect! See here: http://duāt.wordpress.com/2008/01/

[1] I did not find it in the index of ad-Daylamī, *Firdaws ul-Akhbār* so Allāh knows best, a similar hadīth will soon be mentioned narrated from a man from Banu Sulaym.

[2] In *al-Firdaws*, vol.1, p.382, no.1535, al-'Allāmah, al-Muhaqqiq, al-Albānī said in *ad-Da'īfah*, vol.4, pp.191-192, no.1698: *Mawdū'* (a fabricated report): narrated by Abū Nu'aym in *Akhbār Asbahān*, vol.2, p.42 and ad-Daylamī in *al-Musnad*, vol.1, p.1, no.44 (abridged) from 'Anbasah bin 'AbdurRahmān al-Qurashī from 'Abdullāh bin Abi'l-Aswad al-Asbahānī from Ibn 'Umar in a *marfū'* form. Within the biography of this 'AbdurRahmān there is neither a *jarh* nor a *ta'dīl* mentioned of him, and 'Anbasah bin 'AbdurRahmān al-Qurashī has been accused of lying. The hadīth has been mentioned in *al-Fath ul-Kabīr* by al-Hasan bin Sufyān and ad-Daylamī in *Musnad ul-Firdaws* from Ibn 'Umar and in *al-Gharā'ib ul-Multaqah min Musnad il-Firdaws* it has been highlighted has having a defect due to this 'Anbasah being in the chain of transmission. Shaykh al-Albānī stated in *Da'īf ul-Jāmi'*, p.18, no.111: *"mawdū'."* I say: it is mentioned in *al-Kanz*, no.14887 by al-Hasan bin Sufyān.

«اتقوا أبواب السلطان و حواشيها فإن أقرب الناس منها أبعدهم من الله و من آثر سلطانا على الله جعل الله الفتنة في قلبه ظاهرة باطنة و أذهب عنه الورع و تركه حيران»

"Fear the doors of the rulers and its surroundings for the closest people to them are the furthest from Allāh. Whoever follows a ruler before Allāh will have fitna in his heart openly and inwardly and wara' (scrupulous piety and caution) will depart from him."

Ibn 'Asākir reported from Ibn 'Abbās ﵄ who said: the Messenger of Allāh ﷺ said:

« سيكون قوم بعدي من أمتي، يقرؤون القرآن، ويتفقهون في الدين، يأتيهم الشيطان، فيقول: لو أتيتم السلطان، فأصلح من دنياكم، واعتزلوهم بدينكم! ولا يكون ذلك، كما لا يجتنى من القتاد، إلا الشوك، كذلك لا يجتنى من قربهم إلا الخطايا ».

"There will be a people[1] after me from my Ummah who will read the Qur'ān and gain understanding of the deen. Shaytān will come to them and say 'If only you were to go to the ruler and

[1] The word "qawm" (people) is not found in manuscript 'b'.

partake from their worldly riches and then leave them with your deen (in tact)', but this will not be, just as thorns do not bring forth anything except thorns. Likewise, their closeness to the rulers does not bring anything forth except sin."[1]

Hannād bin us-Sirrī reported in *az-Zuhd* from 'Ubayd bin 'Umayr ﷺ[2] that the Messenger of Allāh ﷺ said:

«ما ازداد رجل من السلطان قربا الا ازداد من الله بعدا»

"A man does not increase his closeness to the ruler except that he increases his distance from Allāh."[3,1]

---

[1] Al-Albānī said after ascribing the hadīth to Ibn 'Asākir: "da'īf", see *Da'īf ul-Jāmi'*, p.486, no.3313.

[2] Ibn Qatādah al-Laythī al-Makkī, an admonisher and commentator of the Qur'ān who was born during the time of the Prophet ﷺ. He narrated from his father, from 'Umar ibn al-Khattāb and from Abū Dharr. Those who narrated from him were: 'Atā bin Abī Rabāh, 'Amru bin Dīnār and a group of scholars. Adh-Dhahabī said: "he was from the thiqāt of the tā'bīn and he was of the Imāms of Makkah. He used to remind the people and attend the gatherings of Ibn 'Umar, he died in the year 74 AH." Ibn Qutaybah said about him in *al-Ma'ārif*, p.434: "he died around the time Ibn 'Abbās died in 68 AH" and Allāh knows best. For his biography refer to: *Tabaqāt Ibn Sa'd*, vol.5, p.463; *Tārīkh ul-Bukhārī*, vol.5, p.455; Ibn Qutaybah, *al-Ma'ārif*, p.434; *al-Marifah wa't-Tārīkh*, vol.2, p.24; *al-Hilyah*, vol.3, p.266; see the margins of *as-Siyar*, vol.4, p.156

[3] In manuscript 'b' it states: إلا ازداد عندالله بعداً

Ad-Daylamī reported from Anas ﷺ who said: the Messenger of Allāh ﷺ said:

«من تقرب من ذي سلطان ذراعاً تباعد الله منه باعاً»

"Whoever gains nearness to one who possesses authority by an armspan Allāh will distance the person from him by a long distance."[2,3]

Ad-Daylamī reported from Abi'd-Dardā' ﷺ who said: the Messenger of Allāh ﷺ said:

«من مشى إلى سلطان جائر طوعاً من ذات نفسه، تملقاً إليه بلقائه، والسلام عليه، خاض نار جهنم بقدر خطاه، إلى أن يرجع من عنده إلى منزله فإن مال إلى هواه، أو شد على عضده لم يحلل به من الله لعنة إلا كان عليه مثلها، ولم يعذب في النار بنوع من العذاب، إلا عذب بمثله»

"Whoever walks to an oppressive unjust ruler, out of his own accord, flattering him when he meets and greets him, he will be thrown into

---

[1] In *Da'īf ul-Jāmi'*, p.722, no.4995 it has additional words in it and al-Albānī ascribes it to Hannād in a *mursal* form. The hadīth is also to be found in *az-Zuhd*, vol.1, p.327 and also in Wakī', *az-Zuhd*, vol.1, p.406, al-Albānī stated: "da'īf". I say: the wording is that of Abū Nu'aym, in *al-Hilyah*, vol.3, p.274.

[2] In manuscript 'a' the wordings تباعد عند الله منه ذراعاً

[3] He mentioned the hadīth in *Kanz ul-'Ammāl*, no.6291.

the Hellfire according to the number of his steps - until he returns from the ruler to his abode, and if he leans towards his (the ruler's) evil-desires, or clings to his arm, the curse from Allah as a result will not be released except that it will as it (the clinging) was, and he will not be punished in the Fire with a type of punishment except that it will be its like."[1,2]

Abu'sh-Shaykh reported from Ibn 'Umar ﵄ who said: the Messenger of Allāh ﷺ said:

«من قرأ القرآن وتفقه في الدين ثم أتى صاحب سلطان طمعاً لما في يديه طبع الله على قلبه، وعذب كل يوم بلونين من العذاب، لم يعذب به قبل ذلك»

"Whoever reads the Qur'ān and gains understanding of the deen and then goes to the companion of the ruler aspiring for what the ruler has in his hands, Allāh will seal his heart and punish him with

[1] In manuscript 'b' the wording is slightly different where it says instead: "*lam yahillu bihi min Allāh*".

[2] The author of *al-Kanz* ascribes it to him, no.14954 and with the same meaning it is found in some abridged hadīth see as-Sakhāwī, *al-Maqāsid ul-Husnah*, no.1188 and al-Albānī, *Da'īf ul-Jāmi'*, no.5859.

two times the punishment which he had not been punished with before that."[1]

Al-Hākim reported in his *Tārīkh* from Mu'ādh ﷺ who said: the Messenger of Allāh ﷺ said:

«من قرأ القرآن وتفقه في الدين ثم أتى صاحب سلطان طمعاً لما في يديه خاض بقدر خطاه في نار جهنم»

"Whoever reads the Qur'ān, gains understanding of the deen and then goes to a ruler aspiring for what the ruler has in his hands[2] *will be thrown into Hellfire depending upon the extent of his sin."*[3]

Al-Bayhaqī reported from a man from Banī Sulaym who said: the Messenger of Allāh ﷺ said:

«إياكم وأبواب السلطان»

"Beware of the doors of the ruler!"[4]

---

[1] *Al-Kanz*, nos.29068-29069

[2] This is an addition found in manuscript 'b' but is not found in manuscript 'a'.

[3] The author of *Kanz ul-'Ammāl* ascribes it to him, no.29069

[4] I did not detect it in his *as-Sunan al-Kubrā*, it maybe in *Shu'b ul-Īmān*, and I found it in there in vol.7, p.48, no.9405 and he indicated that the obscure person (from Banī Sulaym) is Abu'l-'A'war as-Sulamī. Al-Haythamī said in *al-Majma'*, vol.5,

Ad-Daylamī reported from 'Ali who said: the Messenger of Allāh ﷺ said:

«إياكم ومجالسة السلطان، فإنه ذهاب الدين، وإياكم ومعونته فإنكم لا تحمدون أمره»

"Beware of sitting with the ruler, for it takes way the deen and beware of supporting him and beware praising his affair."[12]

Ibn Abī Shaybah reported, as did at-Tabarānī, from Ibn 'Abbās ﷺ who said: the Messenger of Allāh ﷺ said:

---

p.249: "it was reported by at-Tabarānī and its men (narrators) are men of the sahīh." Shaykh al-Albānī said in *al-Ahādīth as-Sahīhah*, vol.3, pp.252-253, no.1253:

> It is reported by ad-Daylamī, vol.1, p.2, no.345 via at-Tabarānī and Ibn Mandah in *al-Ma'rifah*, vol.2, p.62, no.2, and Ibn 'Asākir, vol.13, p.232, no.1 from 'Ubayd bin Ya'īsh: Muhammad bin Fudayl narrated to us from Ismā'īl from Qays from Abu'l-A'war as-Sulamī in a *marfū'* form. Then Ibn Mandah reported it via Yahyā bin Zakariyya from Ismā'īl.

I say: this *isnād* is sahīh and all of its narrators are *thiqāt* and Abu'l-A'war his name is 'Amru bin Sufyān, he is differed over as Ibn 'Asākir stated, however his companionship (of the Prophet) is verified by a group of scholars including Imām Muslim.

[1] In manuscript 'b' it says: لا تجدون

[2] I neither found it in *Musnad ul-Firdaws* nor *Kanz ul-'Ammāl* and Allāh knows best.

«إنها ستكون أمراء تعرفون، وتنكرون فمن ناوأهم نجا، ومن اعتزلهم سلم، أو كاد، ومن خالطهم هلك».

"There will be leaders who you will know and reject, whoever stays away from them will be safe and whoever mixes with them will be destroyed."[1]

Al-Bayhaqī[2] reported from 'Ali bin Abī Tālib ﷺ who said:

«اتقوا أبواب السلطان»

"Fear the doors of the ruler."

In *al-Firdaws* from the hadīth of 'Ali ﷺ in a *marfū'* form:

«أفضل التابعين من أمتي من لا يقرب أبواب السلاطين»

"The best tābi'īn (successors) from my Ummah is the one who does not go near the doors of the rulers."[3]

Al-Bayhaqī reported from Ibn Mas'ūd ﷺ who said:

---

[1] The author of *al-Kanz*, no.14404 ascribes it to Ibn Abī Shaybah only.

[2] In *ash-Shu'b*, vol.7, p.49, no.9409, see *al-Majma'*, vol.1, p.324 and at-Tabarānī, vol.10, p.161 and vol.19, p.156.

[3] I neither found it in *al-Firdaws* by ad-Daylamī nor in *Fihrus Kanz il-'Ammāl* and Allāh knows best.

«إن على أبواب السلطان فتناً كمبارك الإبل، لا تصيبون من دنياهم شيئاً[1] إلا أصابوا من دينكم مثله»

"At the doors of the ruler is fitan (a tribulation) like the kneeling of a camel. You will not be affected by their dunya except that your deen will be affected in the like manner."[2]

Ad-Dārimī reported in his *Musnad* from Ibn Mas'ūd ﷺ that he said:

"Whoever wants to honour his deen then let him not visit a ruler or seclude himself with women and not argue with the people of desires."[3]

Al-Bukhārī reported in his *Tārīkh*, as did Ibn Sa'd in *at-Tabaqāt* from Ibn Mas'ūd ﷺ who said:

"A man visits the ruler and has his deen and when he leaves he goes with nothing."[4]

Ibn Sa'd reports in *at-Tabaqāt* from Salamah bin Nabīt who said: "I said to my father, and he had witnessed the Prophet ﷺ, seen him and heard from

---

[1] This word "shay'an" is an addition within manuscript 'b'.

[2] In *ash-Shu'b*, vol.7, p.49, no.9412.

[3] In the *Sunan* in the chapter entitled *'al-'Ilm al-Khashiyyah wa taqwa Allāh'*, vol.1, p.102, no.301 in manuscript 'b': *'al-'Umarā'* [The Rulers].

[4] It is found in the biography of Shabramah bin at-Tufayl, vol.6, p.208.

him: 'O my father if you were to go to this ruler would you afflict yourself and your people?' He replied, 'Yes, for I fear that I sit in a gathering with them which will make me enter the Hellfire.'"[1]

Ad-Dārimī reported from Ibn Mas'ūd ﷺ that he said:

"Whoever seeks knowledge for four (matters) enters the fire: to compete with the 'Ulama, to argue with the foolish, so that people's faces turn to him or so that he can use it to take from the rulers."[2]

Ibn Mājah[3] and al-Bayhaqī[1] reported from Ibn Mas'ūd ﷺ who said: I heard your Prophet ﷺ say,[1]

---

[1] In *at-Tabaqāt*, vol.6, p.30 the wording is slightly different in some of it.

[2] In *Kitāb ul-'Ilm, 'Bāb: at-Tawbīkh liman yutlub al-'Ilm li ghayrillāh'*, vol.1, p.115, no.367 and within the isnad is a man who is not named. I say: its meaning in a *marfū'* form without the last sentence of the hadīth from the hadīth of Abū Hurayrah is authentic as reported by Ibn Mājah in *Kitāb ul-'Ilm, 'Bāb Intifā' bi'l-'Ilm wa'l-'Amal bihi'*, vol.1, p.93; Ahmad, *Musnad*, vol.2, p.338; Ibn Hibbān, *Mawārid udh-Dhamān*, no.89; Ibn 'AbdulBarr, *al-Jāmi'*, vol.1, p.190; al-Hākim, *al-Mustadrak*, vol.1, p.85; al-Khatīb al-Baghdādī, *Iqtidā' al-'Ilm al-'Amal*, no.102. al-Albānī authenticated it in three works: in his *takhrīj* of al-Khatīb al-Baghdādī's *Iqtidā'*; in *Sahīh at-Targhīb wa't-Tarhīb*, nos.102, 105 and also in *Sahīh ul-Jāmi'*, vol.5, p.272, no.6030.

[3] *Kitāb ul-'Ilm, 'Bāb Intifā' bi'l-'Ilm wa'l-'Amal bihi'*, vol.1, p.95, no.257 and similar to it without the mention of Ibn Mas'ūd at the beginning can be found in *Kitāb uz-*

Zuhd, *'Bāb: al-Lahum bi'd-Dunya'*, vol.2, p.1375, no.4106. Al-Buṣayrī stated in *az-Zawā'id*:

> "Its isnād is da'īf for it contains Nahshal bin Sa'īd and it has been said that he reports that which is rejected (manākīr) and rather, it is has been said that he reports fabricated narrations (mawdū'āt)."

[1] In *ash-Shu'b*, no.1888. As for Nahshal bin Sa'īd bin Wardān, then Ishāq bin Rahawayh and Abū Dāwūd at-Tayalisī stated about him: "*kadhdhāb* (a prolific liar)!" Abū Hātim and an-Nasā'ī said about him: "*Matrūk*" and Ibn Ma'īn said "he is nothing!" And one time said "da'īf" and on another occasion said "he is not thiqah (trustworthy)." Ibn Hajar said: "he is *matrūk* and Ishāq bin Rahawayh deemed him to be a liar." See al-'Uqaylī, *ad-Du'afā al-Kabīr*, vol.4, pp.309-310; Ibn 'Adiyy, *al-Kāmil*, vol.7, pp.2521-2522; adh-Dhahabī, *al-Mīzān*, vol.4, p.274; Ibn Hajar, *at-Taqrīb*, vol.2, p.307; Ibn Hajar, *at-Tahdhīb*, vol.10, pp.479-480. Another group of Muhaddithīn weakened the hadīth and they can be seen in the last reference just cited. Al-Albānī said in his commentary to *al-Mishkāt*, vol.1, p.88 after transmitting some of the statements of the *huffādh* about Nahshal: However, al-Busayrī mentions in *az-Zawā'id*, folio 20, p.1, that the hadīth has a supporting narration in the hadīth of Anas." I say: it contains Yazeed ar-Raqāshī who is da'īf, so if there was a supporting hadīth for it the hadīth of Zayd bin Thābit which is reported by Ibn Mājah, no.4105 would take priority because its *sanad* is *sahīh*. Ahmad also reports the same hadīth however the two haeeth have similar meanings and the one which has the closest wording is the hadīth of Ibn 'Umar reported by al-Hākim, vol.4, pp.328-329 about which al-Hākim said: "the isnād is sahīh" and adh-Dhahabī commented on it saying: "it contains Abū 'Aqīl Yahyā bin al-Mutawakkil and he has been weakened."

Al-Albānī however did not realise that in another place the hadīth was mentioned as found in *al-Mustadrak*, vol.2, p.443 and within *at-Takhlīs* by al-Hāfidh adh-Dhahabī and was silent about when al-Hākim said: "the isnād is sahīh" and did not

«من جعل الهموم هما واحدا، هم آخرته، كفاه الله هم دنياه ومن تشعبت به الهموم في أحوال الدنيا لم يبال الله في أي أودیتها هلك»

"Whoever makes his concern one concern, that being the Hereafter, then Allāh will suffice him in regards to the concerns of the dunya. And whoever is split by following the concerns of the dunya, Allāh will not be concerned about which of those things He destroys the person in."

Ibn Abī Shaybah[2] reported from Hudhayfah bin al-Yamān ﷺ[3] who said:

---

comment on this. I then found the hadīth of Ibn Mas'ūd ﷺ with the wording of the author (i.e. as-Suyūtī) in a *marfū'* form as reported by al-'Uqaylī, *ad-Du'afā'*, vol.4, pp.309-310; Ibn 'Adiyy, *al-Kāmil*, vol.7, pp.2521-2522 – who deemed the narration as being unreliable as did Abū Nu'aym in *al-Hilyah*, vol.2, p.105, who said "a strange hadīth from al-Aswad and none have elevated it to the Prophet (ﷺ) except ad-Dahhāk, and none narrated it from him except Nahshal." The like of the hadīth is also found in *Mursal* of Ibn ul-Munkadir, vol.3, p.151 and it is also reported by al-Ājurrī in *Akhlāq ul-'Ulama*, p.108 and also in *'Ilal ul-Hadīth* by Ibn Abī Hātim ar-Rāzī, no.1859. Shaykh al-Albānī deemed the hadīth of Ibn Mas'ūd to be *hasan* as is found in *Sahīh ul-Jāmi'*, vol.5, p.279, no.6065. At-Tabrīzī in *Mishkāt ul-Masābīh*, vol.1, p.88, no.264 ascribes it to al-Bayhaqī in *Shu'b ul-Īmān* and deems it to be a saying of Ibn 'Umar, so Allāh knows best. As-Sakhāwī in *al-Maqāsid*, no.884 ascribes it to him also (i.e. al-Bayhaqī) however deems it as a saying of Ibn Mas'ūd.

[1] In manuscript 'b' it says: "I heard the Prophet..."

[2] I have not been able to detect it up until now.

[3] Hudhayfah bin al-Yamān Abū 'Abdullāh one of the allies of the Ansār and of the notables of the Muhājirīn, his father was al-Yamān and his name was Husayl, a

"Beware! Let no man from among you walk even a handspan towards the one who possesses authority."

Ibn Abī Shaybah reported,[1] as did Abū Nu'aym in *al-Hilyah*,[2] from Hudhayfah ﷺ who said:

"Beware of the positions of fitan!" It was said 'And what are the positions of fitan?' Hudhayfah replied: *"The gates of the rulers, for one of you may enter to see a ruler and believe his lies and say that which is not (truly) in himself."*

Ibn 'Asākir reported from Abū Umāmah al-Bāhilī who said: the Prophet ﷺ said:

---

companion who was martyred at Uhud. Many of the *tābi'īn* (successors) narrated hadīth from Hudhayfah and in al-Bukhārī there is a hadīth wherein Hudhayfah states *"The people used to ask the Messenger of Allāh about the good but I used to ask about the evil for fear of falling into it."* He died at the beginning of the Khilāfah of 'Ali ﷺ in the year 36 AH. See *Tabaqāt Ibn Sa'd*, vol.6, p.15, vol.7, p.317; al-Bukhārī, *Tārīkh ul-Kabīr*, vol.3, p.95; *Hilyat ul-Awliyā'*, vol.1, pp.270-283; Ibn 'AbdulBarr, *al-Istī'āb*, vol.1, p.334; adh-Dhahabī, *Asad ul-Ghābah*, vol.1, p.468; adh-Dhahabī, *as-Siyar*, vol.2, pp.361-369; Ibn Hajar, *al-Isābah*, vol.2, p.223; Ibn ul-'Imād, *Shadharāt udh-Dhahab*, vol.4, pp.96-106.

[1] I found it in al-Bayhaqī, *ash-Shu'b*, vol.7, p.50, no.9413

[2] Abū Nu'aym, *al-Hilyah*, vol.1, p.277

«أبعد الخلق من الله، رجل يجالس الأمراء، فما قالوا من جور صدقهم عليه»

"The furthest creation from Allāh is the man who sits with the leaders and believes whatever evil they say to him."[1]

Al-Bayhaqī reported from Wahb ibn Munabbih[2] that Atā' said:

> *"Beware of the gates of the ruler! For at the gates of the ruler are tribulations (fitan) like the kneeling places of the camels and you will not achieve any of their dunya except by them taking its like in worth from your deen."*[3]

---

[1] I have not been able to detect this hadīth.

[2] He is Wahb bin Munabbih bin Kāmil al-Imām al-'Allāmah al-Ikhbārī Abū 'Abdullāh al-Yamānī, he was born in the year 34 AH. He narrated from Ibn 'Abbās, Jābir and Ibn 'Umar and those who narrated from him were: 'Amru bin Dīnār, his two sons and many others. He was well-versed in the Jewish texts (Isrā'īliyāt) from the scriptures of the Jews and Christians. His narrations in the *Musnad* are few and he died in the year 114 AH. For biographies of him refer to: Ibn Sa'd, *at-Tabaqāt*, vol.5, p.543; Bukhārī, *at-Tārīkh*, vol.8, p.164; Abū Nu'aym, *al-Hilyah*; Ibn Khallikān, *Wafayāt ul-A'yān*, vol.6, p.37; adh-Dhahabī, *Tadhkirat ul-Huffādh*, vol.1, p.95; adh-Dhahabī, *as-Siyar*, vol.4, p.544; Ibn Kathīr, *al-Bidāyah wa'n-Nihāyah*, vol.9, p.276; Ibn Hajar, *Tahdhīb ut-Tahdhīb*, vol.11, p.166 and also within many other sources.

[3] In *ash-Shu'b*, vol.7, p.49, no.9408 and it has an addition at the end of it and it was narrated by Abū Nu'aym in *al-Hilyah*, vol.4, pp.29-30 and this is what Ibn 'Asākir also reported in *at-Tārīkh*, vol.17, p.1480 as is found within the margins of adh-

Ibn Abī Shaybah[1] and al-Bayhaqī[2] reported from Salamah bin Qays who said: 'I met Abū Dharr and he said:

> 'O Salamah bin Qays! Three (things) are to be preserved: that you do not combine two wives (in the same house) for you will not be able to be just even if you tried; do not work to gain charity (from people) for the one who lives off charity increases and decreases and do not surround the one who possesses authority for you will not gain anything at all from their dunya except that they would have taken more from your deen.'

Dhahabī, *as-Siyar*, vol.4, p.549. I also found it in al-Ājurrī but in a longer form in *Akhlāq ul-'Ulama*, p.108.

[1] I did not come across it.

[2] Up to now I have not come across it.

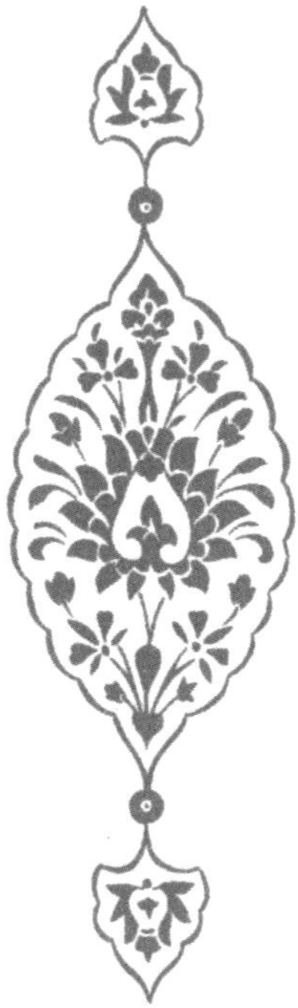

CHAPTER 2

The majority of the 'Ulama from the Salaf, and the recitifiers from the Khalaf, view that these ahādīth and āthār are to be taken in their absolute sense, whether a person is summoned to the rulers or not and whether he is summoned for a religious benefit or otherwise. Sufyān ath-Thawrī stated:

> "If they (the rulers) summon you to recite ***"Qul huwa Allāhu Ahad"*** for them, do not go."

Reported by al-Bayhaqī, as has preceded.[1] Abū Nu'aym reported in *al-Hilyah* from Maymūn bin Mihrān that:

> 'Abdullāh bin 'AbdulMālik bin Marwān arrived in Madeenah and sent his Hājib (chamberlain) to fetch Sa'īd bin al-Musayyib.[2] The

---

[1] This has been mentioned prior, reported from Hammād bin Salamah as found in al-Mizzī's *Tahdhīb ul-Kamāl*, vol.1, p.327.

[2] Ibn Hazn bin 'Amru al-Makhzūmī Abū Muhammad al-Qurashī, the scholar of the people of Madeenah and the master of the Successors (Tābi'īn) of his era. He was born in the first two years of the Khilāfah of 'Umar ﷺ, and he saw 'Umar ﷺ and heard from 'Uthmān, 'Ali, Zayd bin Thābt and the likes of them. Those who narrated from him include Humayd bin 'AbdurRahmān, 'Amru bin Dīnār, Ismā'īl bin Umayyah and a group. He was of those who were prominent in knowledge and action and possessed sternness for the truth. He died in 94 AH.

Refer to *Tabaqāt Ibn Sa'd*, vol.5, p.119; *Tārīkh ul-Bukhārī*, vol.3, p.510; *al-Ma'rifah wa't-Tārīkh*, vol.1, p.468; *al-Hilyah*, vol.2, p.161; *Wafayāt ul-A'yān*, vol.2, p.375;

said to Sa'īd: "Answer the summons of the leader of the believers!" Sa'īd responded: "What does he want?" The chamberlain said: "So that you can speak with him." Sa'īd replied: "I am not of those who speak with him." The chamberlain returned and informed 'Abdullāh and he said: "leave him."[1]

Al-Bukhārī stated in his *Tārīkh*:

> I heard Ādam bin Abī Iyyās say: "I witnessed Hammād bin Salamah say, when he was summoned by the ruler: 'Go to those?! No, by Allāh I will not do it!'"[2]

Al-Khatīb reported about Hammād bin Salamah:

> Some of the Caliphs sent a courier to fetch him saying to him: "an issue has come up so come to us so that we may ask you about it." Hammād said to the courier: "Tell him: we have come across a people who do not go to anyone due to hadīth which have reached

---

Tahdhīb ul-Kamāl, p.505; *Tadhkirat ul-Huffādh*, p.51; *al-'Ibar*, vol.1, p.110; *as-Siyar*, vol.4, p.217; *al-Bidāyah wa'n-Nihāyah*, vol.9, p.99; *Tahdhīb ut-Tahdhīb*, vol.4, p.84; *Tabaqāt ul-Huffādh*, p.17 by as-Suyūtī; *Shadharāt udh-Dhahab*, vol.1, p.102.

[1] Vol.2, p.169. The story is very long and the classifier (Imām as-Suyūtī) abridged it out of necessity for what is to be extracted from the report, he did this often ﷺ.

[2] I found this statement in a copy of the manuscript of *Tahdhīb ul-Kamāl*, vol.1, p.327 by al-Mizzī, with the words *"...Beautify my beard with red for those?! No, by Allāh I will not do it!"* It is as if the author (as-Suyūtī) transmitted from here.

them, so if you have any issue write it down on a scroll (Ruq'ah), send it to us and we will answer it."

Abu'l-Hasan bin Fahr[1] relayed in his book *Fadā'il Mālik* from'Abdullāh bin Rāfi' and others who said:

> Hārūn ar-Rashīd arrived in Madeenah and sent al-Barmakī to fetch Mālik and to say to him: "Bring me the book which you have compiled so that I can hear it from you." Mālik said to al-Barmakī: "Convey my salām to him and say to him: knowledge has to be visited and does not visit (others)." Al-Barmakī returned back to Hārūn ar-Rashīd and said to him: "O leader of the believers! Convey to the people of al-'Irāq that you approached Malik and he opposed you! Be firm with him so that he comes to you." When Mālik was summoned again he said: "Tell him: O leader of the believers do not be the first to waste knowledge as Allāh will waste you."[2]

---

[1] 'Ali bin al-Hasan bin Muhammad bin al-'Abbās, the Mālikī jurist. In the East he heard from a large group of scholars such as adh-Dhalā'ī and al-Muhallab bin Abī Safrah. Al-Muhallab said: "I met him in Egypt and Makkah and I did not meet the likes of him, he authored much on the virtues of Mālik bin Anas." Refer to Ibn Farhūn, *ad-Dībāj al-Madhhab*, vol.1, p.202.

[2] I found that al-Hāfidh Ibn 'Asākir relayed this story with his chain of transmission in his book *Juz Kashf ul-Mughatta fi Fadl il-Muwatta'*, pp.8-9. In the longer version of the story the one who said to Hārūn ar-Rashīd: "convey to the people of al-'Irāq

Ghunjār relayed in his *Tārīkh* from Ibn Munayyar that:

> The Sultān of Bukhārā sent a messenger for Muhammad bin Ismā'īl al-Bukhārī saying: "Bring me the books *al-Jāmi'* and *at-Tārīkh* so that I may hear it from you." Al-Bukhārī said to the messenger: "Tell him: I do not belittle knowledge and I do not go to the doors of the rulers. If you have any need then come to me at my Masjid or at my house."[1]

..." was al-Qādī Abū Yūsuf, the jurist. At the end of the story Mālik says: "If knowledge is withheld from the common people for the benefit of the eminent people then Allāh will not bring any benefit in the knowledge for the eminent people." Ma'n bin 'Īsā al-Qazzār ordered him to read it and when Mālik began reading Mālik said to Hārūn ar-Rashīd: "O leader of the believers, I came across the people of knwoledge in our land and they loved humility for knowledge." Hārūn then came down from his throne and sat before Mālik.

[1] The author (as-Suyūtī) ﷺ abridged the story and it is as follows, as stated by adh-Dhahabī in *as-Siyar*, vol.12, p.464: Ghunjār stated in his *Tārīkh*:

> I heard Abū 'Amru Ahmad bin Muhammad al-Muqri' say: I heard Bakr bin Munīr bin Khalīd bin 'Askar say: the ruler of Bukhāra, Prince Khālid bin Ahmad adh-Dhuhalī sent for Muhammad bin Ismā'īl so that he would bring to him his books *al-Jāmi'*, *at-Tārīkh* and others (saying) "so that I could hear them from you (al-Bukhārī)". Imām al-Bukhārī said to the messenger: "I do not belittle knowledge and I do not go to the doors of the rulers. If you have any need then come to me at my Masjid or at my house. If this does not please you then you are the ruler and you can force me to the gathering and then I will have an excuse with Allāh on the Day of Judgement. For I do not hide knowledge based on the saying of the Prophet ﷺ: 'Whoever is asked

Nu'aym bin al-Haysam[1] stated in his famous *Juz*:

[It was narrated to us by Khalaf][2] bin Tamīm from Abū Hamām al-Kalā'ī from al-Hasan,[3] that he walked passed some reciters who were at the gates of the leaders and said to them: do you blister your foreheads, flatten your soles and take the knowledge which you carry

---

about knowledge and hides it will be bridled with a bridle from Hellfire.'" This was the reason for the tension between the two of them.

Refer to *Tārīkh Baghdād*, vol.2, p.33; *Tahdhīb ul-Kamāl*, p.338; *Tabaqāt us-Subkī*, vol.2, pp.232-233; *Muqaddimah Fath ul-Bārī*, p.493; adh-Dhahabī transmitted from al-Hākim with his chain of transmission from Sahl bin Shādhawayh and mentioned a part of the reports of al-Bukhārī and said: "Muhammad bin Ismā'īl had *wara'* and avoided the rulers and did not visit them."

[1] Abū Muhammad, he resided in Baghdād and Ibn Ma'īn said about him: "Sudūq". He has a copy which was compiled by Abu'l-Qāsim al-Baghawī in which he reported from Abū 'Awānah. Hātim bin al-Layth and Mūsā bin Hārūn narrated from him. He died in 228 AH. See Ibn Hajar, *Lisān ul-Mīzān*, vol.6, pp.204-205.

[2] This is dropped from manuscript 'a'.

[3] Al-Hasan bin Abi'l-Hasan Yasār Abū Sa'īd al-Basrī, the prominent Imām and Zāhid. He relayed from 'Imrān bin Husayn, Samurah bin Jundub, Anas and a large body of companions. Those who relayed from him were the likes of Yūnus bin 'Ubayd, Humayd at-Tawīl, Thābit al-Banānī and others. He died in 110 AH. For his biography refer to: *Tabaqāt Ibn Sa'd*, vol.7, p.156; *Tabaqāt Khalīfah*, no.1726; *Tārīkh ul-Bukhārī*, vol.2, p.289; *al-Ma'rifah wa't-Tārīkh*, vol.2, p.32, vol.3, p.338; *al-Hilyah*, vol.2, p.131; *Wafayāt ul-A'yān*, vol.2, p.69; *Tadhkirat ul-Huffādh*, vol.1, p.66; *as-Siyar*, vol.4, pp.563-588; *al-Bidāyah wa'n-Nihāyah*, vol.9, pp.266-268; *Tahdhīb ut-Tahdhīb*, vol.2, p.263; *Tabaqāt ul-Huffādh*, p.28; *Shadharāt udh-Dhahab*, vol.1, p.136.

> on your necks to their doors?! If you were to remain seated in your homes it would be better for you.[1]

Abū Nu'aym reported in *al-Hilyah* from Wuhayb[2] bin al-Warad[3] that he said:

> It has reached us that the 'Ulama are of three types: the scholar who seeks knowledge for the rulers; the scholar who seeks knowledge for the traders and the scholar who seeks knowledge merely for himself and does not want it except that he fears acting without knowledge and hereby causing corruption more than rectification.[4]

Abū Nu'aym reported from Abū Sālih al-Antākī who said:

---

[1] I did not find this quote in the sources that I looked at.

[2] In manuscript 'b': Wahb.

[3] Abū Umayyah, the freed slave of Bani Makhzūm. He met Ā'ishah ﵂ and narrated from Humayd al-A'raj and Ibn ul-Munkadir. Ibn ul-Mubārak, 'AbdurRazzāq and others narrated for them. He was from the 'Ulama who were 'Ubbād (constant worshippers). Ibn Ma'īn said about him: "thiqah". An-Nasā'ī said about him: "there is no problem with him". He died in the year 153 AH. For his biography refer to: *Tabaqāt Ibn Sa'd*, vol.5, p.488; *at-Tārīkh ul-Kabīr*, vol.8, p.177; *al-Ma'rifah wa't-Tārīkh*, vol.1, p.434; *al-Jarh wa't-Ta'dīl*, vol.9, p.34; *al-Hilyah*, vol.8, pp.140-161; *al-'Ibar*, vol.1, p.222; *as-Siyar*, vol.7, pp.198-199; *Tahdhīb ut-Tahdhīb*, vol.11, pp.170-171; al-Khazrījī, *Khulāsatu Tahdhīb il-Kamāl*, p.419; *Shadharāt udh-Dhahab*, vol.1, p.236.

[4] *Al-Hilyah*, vol.8, p.156 – but the "three" and the first sentence is missing from *al-Hilyah* and in its place is: "...the scholar who seeks knowledge in order to gain wealth from traders."

I heard Ibn ul-Mubārak[1] say: "whoever is stingy with regards to knowledge will by tested by three: either by death which will lead to his knowledge disappearing; or due to forgetfulness or due to sticking close to the ruler [and then his knowledge will disappear]."[2]

Al-Khatīb al-Baghdādī stated in his book *Ruwāt Mālik*:

Al-Qādī Abu'l-Qāsim al-Hasan bin Muhammad bin al-Anbārī wrote to me from Egypt saying: Muhammad bin Ahmad bin al-Masūr informed us: al-Miqdām bin Dāqud ar-Ra'īnī informed us: 'Ali bin Ma'bad informed us: Ishāq bin Yahyā informed us from Mālik bin Anas ﵀ that he said: "I came across some ten men from the Successors all saying do not go to them and do not pass by them - meaning the ruler."

---

[1] Shaykh ul-Islām, the scholar of the Zuhhād, Abū 'Abdullāh al-Hāfidh al-Mujāhid, born in 118 AH. He surpassed the horizons in seeking knowledge, waged war, authored works and brought much benefit. His narrations in regards to zuhd and 'ilm are famous that they need not to mentioned. He died in 181 AH. For his biography refer to: al-Bukhārī, *Tārīkh ul-Kabīr*, vol.5, p.212; Ibn Abee Hātim, *Jarh wa't-Ta'dīl*, vol.5, p.179; Abū Nu'aym, *al-Hilyah*, vol.8, p.162; Ibn'AbdulBarr, *al-Intiqā'*, p.132; al-Khatīb, *Tārīkh Baghdād*, vol.10, p.152; the margins of *as-Siyar*, vol.8, p.378.

[2] This is missing from manuscript 'b'.

Ibn Bākuwayh ash-Shīrāzī[1] stated in *Akhbār us-Sūfiyyah*:

Salāmah bin Ahmad at-Takrīnī narrated to us: Ya'qūb bin Ishāq informed us: 'Ubaydullāh bin Muhammad al-Qurashī informed us saying: we were with Sufyān ath-Thawrī in Makkah and a letter came to him from his family in Kūfah which read: "it has reached the extent that we are in need to fry date stones and eat them." Sufyān cried. Then one of his companions said: "O Abū 'Abdullāh, if you were to pass by the ruler you would gain what you want!" Sufyān said; "By Allāh I do not ask for the dunya from the one who

[1] The righteous Imām, Muhaddith and Shaykh of the Sūfīs, Abū 'Abdullāh. He was born in 340 AH and sought hadīth and travelled for it, he heard from Muhammad bin Khafīf az-Zāhid, Ibn 'Adiyy, al-Ismā'īlī, al-Qatī'ī and others. Those who narrated from him were Abu'l-Qāsim al-Qushayrī, 'AbdulWahhāb ath-Thaqafī and others. He has some works which he authored and classified. He died in 428 AH (1037 CE), ﷺ. For his biography refer to Ibn as-Sam'ānī, *al-Ansāb*, vol.2, p.54; Ibn ul-Athīr, *al-Lubāb*, vol.1, p.113; *al-Mushtabah*, vol.1, p.44; *al-'Ibar*, vol.3, p.167; *as-Siyar*, vol.17, p.544 – all works by adh-Dhahabī; as-Safadī, *al-Wāfī bi'l-Wafayāt*, vol.3, p.322; *Shadharāt udh-Dhahab*, vol.3, p.242; *Hidāyat ul-'Ārifīn*, vol.2, p.65.

[TN] early Sufism was essentially free of much of the later erroneous practices and beliefs which has shaped the later meaning of the term, indeed nowadays Sufism is seen by many people in the west as being no different to a form of mystic yoga (!) - as people who are overtly non-Muslim ascribe to Sufism in the West today. Not to mention a whole host of practices and beliefs which are far from the beliefs held by the Salaf. A Sūfī therefore, in the period after the Salaf and before the later void Sūfī beliefs and practices, was viewed as being a Zāhid and it shared the same meaning as zuhd.

possesses it (i.e. Allāh), so how can I ask it from the one who do not possess it."

'AbdulWāhid narrated to us: Ahmad bin Muhammad bin Hamdūn informed us: Abū 'Īsā al-Anbārī informed us: Fath bin Shukhruf informed us: 'Abdullāh bin Hasan informed us from Sufyān ath-Thawrī:

"Fortify yourselves from the sons of the worldly life by avoiding giving them salāms."

'Abdullāh bin Muhammad bin Ja'far narrated to us: Ibn Hassān informed us: Ahmad bin Abi'l-Hiwārī informed us saying:

I said to Abū Sulaymān: "Do you oppose the 'Ulama?" He became angry and said: "I saw a scholar go to the door of the ruler and take from their money."[1] I heard 'AbdulWāhid bin Bakr say: I heard Muhammad bin Dāwud ad-Dīnawarī say: I heard Ahmad bin as-Salt say: I man went to Bishr bin al-Hārith[2] and said to him: 'O

---

[1] In manuscript 'b': "...take from his money (dirāhimihi)."

[2] He is Bishr bin al-Hārith bin 'AbdurRahmān, Abū Nasr al-Marwazī, the Imām, Muhaddith, Zāhid, Rabbānī. He was also known as "al-Hāfī" and was born in 152 AH and took from Mālik, Shurayk, Hammād bin Salamah, Fudayl ibn 'Iyyād, Ibn ul-Mubārak and a number of other notables. Those who narrated from him include: Ahmad ad-Dawraqī, Muhammad bin Yūsuf al-Jawharī and a group of others like them. He was a leader in *wara'* and *ikhlās*. He died in 227 AH ﷺ. For his biography refer to: *Tabaqāt Ibn Sa'd*, vol.7, p.342; *al-Jarh wa't-Ta'dīl*, vol.2, p.356; *Hilyat ul-Awliya*, vol.8, p.336-360; *Tārīkh Baghdād*, vol.7, p.67; *Sifat us-Safwah*, vol.2,

Master! The ruler requests the righteous (to visit him), do you view that I should hide?' Bishr replied: 'Move from in front of me, it is not permitted and they will throw you on us.'

Al-Āmidī stated: Abu'l-'Abbās narrated to me saying:

I heard that Tāhir bin 'Abdullāh bin Tāhir arrived from Khurasān during the lifetime of his father and wanting to make Hajj. He stayed at the house of Ishāq bin Ibrāhīm[1] and Ishāq directed him to the 'Ulama, so Ishāq gathered them so that Tāhir could see them and read to them. The people of hadīth and fiqh attended and Ibn al-A'rābī also attended as did Abū Nasr, the companion of al-

---

pp.183-190; *Wafayāt ul-A'yān*, vol.1, pp.274-277; *al-'Ibar*, vol.1, p.399; *as-Siyar*, vol.1-, pp.469-477; *Marāt ul-Janān*, vol.2, p.92; *al-Bidāyah wa'n-Nihāyah*, vol.10, pp.297-299; *Tahdhīb ut-Tahdhīb*, vol.1, p.444; *an-Nujūm az-Zāhirah*, vol.2, pp.249-250; *Shadharāt udh-Dhahab*, vol.2, pp.60-62.

[1] He is the Imām, the Hāfidh, the Mujtahid, he was born in 161 AH and heard from Ibn ul-Mubārak, Ibn Wahb, Ibn 'Uyaynah and many others. Al-Bukhārī, Muslim, Abū Dāwud, an-Nasā'ī and others all narrated from him. Imām Ahmad said about him: "I do not know of anyone in the Dunyā who can be compared to Ishāq." He died in 238 AH. For his biography refer to: *at-Tārīkh al-Kabīr*, vol.1, p.379; *al-Jarh wa't-Ta'dīl*, vol.2, pp.209-210; *Hilyat ul-Awliyā*, vol.9, p.234; *Tārīkh Baghdād*, vol.6, pp.245-255; Abū Ya'lā, *Tabaqāt ul-Hanābilah*, vol.1, p.109; *al-Ansāb*, vol.6, pp.56-57; *Wafayāt ul-A'yān*, vol.1, pp.199-201; *Tadhkirat ul-Huffādh*, vol.2, p.433; *as-Siyar*, vol.11, pp.358-383; *Tahdhīb ut-Tahdhīb*, vol.1, pp.216-219; *Shadharāt udh-Dhahab*, vol.2, p.89.

Asma'ī. Abū'Ubayd al-Qāsim bin as-Sallām[1] was invited to attend but he declined the offer saying: "knowledge is sought out." Ishāq became angry at these words and the letter (sent by Imām Abū 'Ubayd). 'Abdullāh bin Tāhir used to send him two thousand Dirhams each month but Ishāq did not hand it over to Abū 'Ubayd, hereby cutting off his sustenance. He wrote to 'Abdullāh bin Tāhir about what happened and 'Abdullāh replied saying: "Abū 'Ubayd has certainly spoken the truth in what he said and I have doubled his sustenance due to this action. So give it to him and then after that give him back everything that he deserves."

Ibn 'Asākir reported, via the route of Ibn Wahb, from 'AbdurRahmān bin Yazīd, saying:

---

[1] The Hāfidh, Mujtahid, the luminary who mastered the arts, he was born in 157 AH and heard Ibn 'Uyaynah, Hushaym, Ibn ul-Mubārak and from a group of others. Those who narrated form him include: Ibn Abī ad-Dunyā, al-Hārith bin Abī Usāmah and some others. He authored some prominent works such as *Gharīb ul-Hadīth, al-Amwāl* and *al-Amthāl.* He died in 224 AH. For a biography of him refer to: *Tabaqāt Ibn Sa'd*, vol.7, p.355; *at-Tārīkh al-Kabīr*, vol.7, p.172; *Tārīkh Baghdād*, vol.12, pp.403-416; *Tadhkirat ul-Huffādh*, vol.1, p.417; *as-Siyar*, vol.10, pp.490-511; *Tahdhīb ut-Tahdhīb*, vol.8, p.315; *Shadharāt udh-Dhahab*, vol.2, pp.54-55 and other sources.

Abū Hāzim narrated to me that Sulaymān bin Hishām bin 'AbdulMalik arrived in Madeenah and sent for Abū Hāzim.[1] So he entered and said: "So I gave salāms while I was resting on my staff. It was said: 'Will you not speak!?' I said: What should I talk about?! I have no need to speak about anything. I only came for the need for which you requested of me and I do not go to all who request me to see them, and if it was not for the fear of your evil I would not come. For I discovered that Ahl ud-Dunyā follow Ahl ul-'Ilm wherever they were, Ahl ul-'Ilm fulfil the needs of the Ahl ud-Dunyā' in this life and the next. Ahl ud-Dunyā' will never be sufficed from the Ahl ul-'Ilm due to their portion of knowledge. Then the times change when Ahl ul-'Ilm begin to follow Ahl ud-Dunyā' wherever they are, and then this leads to tribulation to both

[1] Salamah bin Dīnār, the prominent Imām, the admonisher, the Shaykh of Madeenat un-Nabawiyyah, he was born during the days of Ibn uz-Zubayr and Ibn 'Umar. He relayed from Sahl bin Sa'd, Abū Umāmah, Sa'īd bin al-Musayyib, Umm ud-Dardā', Abū Salamah bin 'AbdurRahmān and a number of others. Those who relayed from him include: Ibn Shihāb, Yazīd bin 'Abdullāh bin al-Hād, 'Amārah bin Ghuzzayah, the two Hammāds, the two Sufyāns and some others. Ibn Ma'īn, Ahmad and Abū Hātim deemed him as *thiqah* and Ibn Khuzaymah stated: "*Thiqah*, there was no one during his time similar to him." For his biography refer to *Tabaqāt Khalīfah*, p.264; *Tārīkh ul-Bukhārī*, vol.2, p.78; *at-Tārīkh as-Saghīr*, vol.2, p.47; *al-Jarh wa't-Ta'dīl*, vol.4, p.159; *Hilyat ul-Awliyā'*, vol.3, p.229; *Tadhkirat ul-Huffādh*, vol.1, p.133; *as-Siyar*, vol.6, pp.96-103; *Tahdhīb ut-Tahdhīb*, vol.4, p.143; *Tahdhīb Tārīkh Ibn 'Asākir*, vol.6, pp.216-228.

sides. Ahl ud-Dunyā' left the portion of knowledge which they possessed when they see Ahl ul-'Ilm going to them. Ahl ul-'Ilm wasted the huge portion of knowledge which was given to them due to following Ahl ud-Dunyā'."[1]

Ibn Abi'd-Dunyā, al-Kharā'itī and Ibn 'Asākir reported from Zam'ah bin Sālih who said:

> Some of the Banī Umayyah wrote to Abū Hāzim that he request his needs unto them. Abū Hāzim wrote back to them saying: 'To proceed: your letter has reached me wherein you ask me to raise my needs unto you, how far is this from occurring! I have raised my needs to my Master (i.e. Allāh) and whatever He gives me I accept and whatever is withheld from me I am pleased with."[2]

Ibn 'Asākir reported, from 'AbdulJabbār bin 'Abdul'Azīz Abī Hāzim from his father from his grandfather that:

> Sulaymān bin 'AbdulMālik entered Madeenah and stayed there for three days, he said: "Is there a man here who has come across the companions of Muhammad ﷺ and can narrate to us?" It was said to him: "Yes indeed, herein is a man who is called Abū Hāzim." Abū

---

[1] I did not find this in *Mukhtasar ut-Tārīkh*.

[2] The like of this is found within to routes reported by Abū Nu'aym in *al-Hilyah*, vol.3, p.237

Hāzim was sent for and he came to him. Sulaymān said to him: "O Abū Hāzim! What is this coarseness? All the faces of Madeenah have come to me yet you do not come to me!? " Abū Hāzim replied: "When the people were on the correct way the leaders were in need of the *'Ulama* and the *'Ulama* would flee with their deen from leaders. Yet when a people from the most humiliated of people saw this they began to seek knowledge so as to go to the rulers with it and those rulers became sufficed from the *'Ulama.* Those people became united on disobedience and they fell and became destroyed. If those *'Ulama,* who humiliated themselves by going to the rulers, maintained their knowledge the rulers would respect them."[1]

Abū Nu'aym and Ibn 'Asākir reported from Yūsuf bin Asbāt who said: Najm informed us that some rulers sent for Abū Hāzim and so he went to unto them and with him was al-Ifrīqī, az-Zuhrī and some others. The ruler said to Abū Hāzim: "Speak O Abū Hāzim!" Abū Hāzim replied: "The best rulers are those who love the *'Ulama* and the worst *'Ulama* are those who love the rulers. In the past, if the rulers sent for the *'Ulama,* the *'Ulama* would not go to them and if they rulers asked the *'Ulama* anything, the *'Ulama* would not make any concessions for the rulers. The rulers used to go to the *'Ulama*

[1] The like of this very long story is found in *Mukhtasar Tārīkh Ibn 'Asākir*, vol.6, pp.219-221 and in *al-Hilyah*, vol.3, pp.234-237.

at their homes and ask them and within this was rectification for both the rulers and the scholars. When some people saw this they said to themselves: 'What is wrong with us that we do not seek knowledge so that we be like those?!' They sought knowledge and then went to the rulers and spoke with them and made concessions for them, then the scholars became destroyed at the hands of the rulers and the rulers at the hands of the scholars."[1]

Ibn 'Asākir from Muhammad bin 'Ajlān al-Madanī who said:

Sulaymān bin Hishām was sent to Abū Hāzim and said to him: "Speak!" Abū Hāzim replied: "I have no need for which to speak, and if it was not that I feared you evil I would not come to you. For certainly the time has come upon us herein the leader request the *'Ulama* who then take from what is in their hands and benefit from it. In that was rectification for both parties. Today however the *'Ulama* request the leaders, lowering themselves before them and desiring what the leaders have in their hands. The leaders say 'They would not seek what is in our hands unless what is within our hands is better than what is between their own hands.' In that is corruption for both parties." Sulaymān bin Hishām then said: "You have spoken the truth (O Abū Hāzim)."

---

[1] The like of this event is reported by Abū Nu'aym in *al-Hilyah*, vol.3, pp.243-244.

[Ibn 'Asākir][1] reports from al-Awzā'ī who said:

'Atā'[2] al-Khurasānī visited Hishām bin 'AbdulMalik[3] and then visited Makhūl. 'Atā' said to Makhūl: "Is there anyone here who can move us?" Meaning by this: is there anyone here who can admonish us? Makhūl said: "Yes, Yazīd bin Maysarah."[4] So Yazīd bin Maysarah was brought forth and 'Atā' said to him: "Move us (with your speech), may Allāh have mercy upon you!" Yazīd replied: "Yes: the '*Ulama* if they knew something they would act on it and they acted on something they would be occupied and if they were occupied they would be lost (i.e. absent due to their occupation) and if they were lost they would be sought-after and if they were sought after they would flee." 'Atā' said: "Repeat this to me." So it

---

[1] This is dropped from Manuscript 'b'.

[2] In Manuscript 'a': al-'Atā'.

[3] In Manuscript 'b': "bin 'Abdul'Azīz" and this is a clear error.

[4] I am more than sure that this refers to Yazīd bin Samurah ar-Rahāwī al-Madhhijī, the Zāhid. He was from Shām and there is a textual discrepancy in the copy. He reported from 'Atā' al-Khurasānī, Yahyā ash-Shaybānī, al-Awzā'ī, al-Hakam bin 'AbdurRahmān. Those who reported from him include: Ibn Wahb, Abū Mashar, Yahyā bin Bakīr, Ibn 'Ā'id, Hishām bin 'Ammār and others. Abū Zur'ah ad-Dimishqī said about him: "He was of the virtuous people and ascetics." Ibn Yūnus said about him: "They did not mention him with a *Jarh* and he is of the generational level of Ibn Wahb and Wakī'." For his biography refer to *Tārīkh ul-Kabīr*, vol.8, p.337; *al-Jarh wa't-Ta'dīl*, vol.9, p.268 and *as-Siyar*, vol.9, p.106. Allāh knows best.

was repeated to 'Atā' and then he went back without meeting up with Hishām.

Al-Khatīb and Ibn 'Asākir reported from Muqātil bin Sālih al-Khurasānī who said:

> I went to visit Hammād bin Salamah and I sat with him when someone knocked on the door. Hammād said: "O servant girl, go and see who that is." She said:[1] "It is the messenger of Muhammad bin Sulaymān al-Hāshimī, the leader of al-Basrah and al-Kūfah." Hammād said: "Say to him that only he can come in." The messenger man came in, gave salāms and presented his book to him and said: "read it." The document read: "In the Name of Allāh, the Most Beneficent, the Most Merciful. From Sulaymān to Hammād bin Salamah. To proceed: An issue has emerged and we need you to come to us so that we can ask you about it." Hammād replied: "O servant girl, bring me the ink." Then Hammād said [to me]:[2] "Turn the document over and write on it the following: to proceed: I have come across the *'Ulama* and they do not go to anyone, so if an issue has come up then come to us, ask us about what has arisen with you! If you come to me, only one person should come and do not come to me with all the kings horses and all the kings men, salām."

[1] In manuscript 'b': 'he said'.

[2] This is missing from manuscript 'b'.

I was sitting with Hammād and then someone knocked on the door, Hammād said: "O servant girl, go and see who this is!" She said: "It is Muhammad bin Sulaymān." Hammād said: "Say to him that he alone should come in." He came in, gave salāms and then sat in front of Hammād and began asking his question and said: "When I looked at you I became full of fear, what is with me?!" Hammād said: "I heard Thābit al-Banānī say: I heard Anas bin Mālik say: I heard Allāh's Messenger ﷺ say: *"If the scholar wants Allāh's Face by his knowledge then everything will be in awe of him and if he wants treasures for his knowledge then he becomes in awe of everything.*""[1] Then he mentioned the rest of the story.

Al-Bayhaqī reported in *Shu'b ul-Īmān* from Bishr al-Hāfī who said:

"What is viler than hearing about a scholar who is being being looked for, than this: 'he is at the gate of the ruler'?"[2]

---

[1] Al-Hāfidh al-'Irāqī stated in *Takhrīj ul-Ihyā*, vol.2, p.145:
This narration is *Mu'dal* and it was relayed by Abu'sh-Shaykh Ibn Hibbān in *Kitāb uth-Thawāb* from the hadīth of Wāthilah bin al-Asqa': *"Whoever fears Allāh then Allāh will make everything fear him and whoever does not fear Allāh then Allāh will make him fear everything."* Al-'Uqaylī in *ad-Du'afā'* relays a similar hadīth from Abū Hurayrah – both reports are *munkar*.
[TN] a Mu'dal report is a hadīth wherein two or more consecutive narrators are missing from a chain of narration.

CHAPTER 3

Al-Ghazālī states in *al-Ihyā'* in the chapter about mixing with the rulers and the ruling of sitting with them and visiting them.[1] Al-Ghazālī stated:

> You should know that unto you are three conditions with regards to the oppressive rulers and workers:
>
> One: which is the worst case - to visit them.
>
> Two: this is less than the first, that they visit you.
>
> Three: which is the safer case, that you stay away from them and you do not see them and they do not see you.[2]

As for the first case: which is visiting them, then this is censured to the utmost in the Shar' and severe warnings have been relayed in the reports and narrations which we will relay in order to know the censure of it in the Shar'. Then we will present what is prohibited, what is permitted and what is disliked. Then a presentation of the ahādīth and āthār which have been mentioned prior. What he (al-Ghazālī) relayed (in *al-Ihyā*) which was not mentioned prior was: Sufyān stated:

---

[2] The likes of this is relayed by Ibn Hibbān with his chain of transmission from al-Fudayl ibn 'Iyyād in *Rawdat ul-'Uqalā'*, p.33 and in *Shu'b ul-Īmān*, p.1858.

[1] *Al-Ihyā'*, az-Zubaydī, *Sharh Ithāf as-Sādah al-Muttaqīn*, vol.6, pp.124-142.

[2] *Al-Ithāf*, vol.6, p.124.

In Jahannam is a valley which is not dwelt in except by the reciters and those who visit the kings.[1]

Al-Awzā'ī[2] said:

There is nothing more hated to Allāh than a scholar who visits a worker (of the ruler).

Ishāq said:

What is viler (Asmaju) than a scholar who when he is visited at his class is not found there so when it is asked where he is, it is said: 'he is with the ruler'.

And I used to hear that he said:

If you see a scholar visiting the ruler then accuse him over your deen. I never ever made such a visit except that I took myself to

---

[1] Ascribed to al-Bayhaqī, *al-Ithāf*, vol.6, p.167.

[2] 'AbdurRahmān bin 'Amru, Shaykh ul-Islām, the scholar of Shām, who was born in 88 AH. He relayed from 'Atā' bin Abī Rabāh, Makhūl, Qatādah and others. Those who relayed from him: Mālik, ath-Thawrī and Ibn ul-Mubārak. He died in 157 AH. For his biography refer to *Tabaqāt Ibn Sa'd*, vol.7, p.488; *al-Ma'rifah wa't-Tārīkh*, vol.2, p.390-397, 408-410; *Hilyat ul-Awliyā'*, vol.6, pp.135-149; *Wafayāt ul-A'yān*, vol.3, pp.127-128; *Tadhkirat ul-Huffādh*, vol.1, pp.178-185; *as-Siyar*, vol.7, p.107-134; *Tahdhīb ut-Tahdhīb*, vol.6, pp.238-242, *Shadharāt udh-Dhahab*, vol.1, pp.241-242.

account after leaving, I blamed myself even though I faced them with harshness and opposition to their desires.

Sa'īd ibn al-Musayyib used to trade in olive oil and said:

"Within this (trade) is sufficiency from those rulers."

Wahb said:

"Those who enter upon the kings are more harmful to the Ummah than gamblers (Muqāmirīn)."

Muhammad bin Maslamah[1] stated:

"Flies upon faeces are better than reciters at the gates of those (rulers)."

---

[1] The long-living Muhaddith Abū Ja'far al-Wāsitī, at-Tayālisī, 178 AH and he narrated in Baghdād from Yazīd bin Hārūn, Abū Jābir Muhammad bin 'AbdulMalik, Abū 'AbdurRahmān al-Maqarrī, Mūsā at-Tawīl. Those who narrated from him are: Abū Ja'far al-Bakhtarī, Muhammad bin Mukhallid al-'Attār, Abū Bakr ash-Shāfi'ī, Ahmad bin Thābit al-Wāsitī and a group of others. Al-Hākim relayed from ad-Dāraqutnī that he said about Muhammad bin Maslamah: "there is no harm in him." Al-Khatīb said: "I saw Abu'l-Qāsim al-Lālikā'ī and al-Hasan bin Muhammad al-Khallāl and they both deemed him to be weak." Al-Khatīb said about him: "He relays some *Manākīr.*" He died in 288 AH. For his biography refer to *Tārīkh Baghdād*, vol.3, pp.305-307; *Mīzān ul-I'tidāl*, vol.4, pp.41-42; *as-Siyar*, vol.13, pp.395-396; *al-Wāfī bi'l-Wafayāt*, vol.5, p.30 and *Lisān ul-Mīzān*, vol.5, pp.432-433.

When az-Zuhrī began to mix with the rulers, one of his brothers in the deen wrote to him saying:

> May Allāh grant us and you safety from tribulations O Abū Bakr. For you have become in a state which requires from those that know you to supplicate for you and ask Allāh to show mercy to you. You have become a big Shaykh and you have bore the blessings of Allāh due to what He has granted you of understanding from His Book and from what He has taught you from the Sunnah of His Prophet ﷺ. It is not like this as Allāh took the covenant from the *'Ulama*.[1] Know that the slightest thing you have commited, and the least thing you have carried, is that you have become familiar with the brutality (*Wihsha*) of the oppressor and you have made easy the way to misguidance by your proximity to those who do not deserve that right. Yet he did not leave the falsehood when he (the ruler) made you close to him. They have taken you as a pole around which to rotate their oppression, and they have taken you as a bridge over which to cross to their calamities, and they have taken you as a ladder on which to ascend to their misguidance. They have used you to put doubt on the *'Ulama* and to assaninate the hearts of the ignorant. Look at how easy it was for them to build up things for you

---

[1] In *al-Ithāf*, vol.6, p.128: Allāh says

"You must make it clear to the people and not conceal it."

{Āl 'Imrān (3): 187}

in comparison to what they have ruined for you. Look at how much they took from you in comparison to what they have corrupted from your deen. What will grant you safety from being among those about whom Allāh says:

﴿ فَخَلَفَ مِنۢ بَعۡدِهِمۡ خَلۡفٌ أَضَاعُواْ ٱلصَّلَوٰةَ وَٱتَّبَعُواْ ٱلشَّهَوَٰتِۖ فَسَوۡفَ يَلۡقَوۡنَ غَيًّا ﴾

"But there came after them successors who neglected prayer and pursued desires..." *{Maryam (19): 59}*?

Indeed, you dealing with One Who knows (i.e. Allāh) and who is preserving things about you and not heedless. Cure your religion as disease has entered it and prepare your provisions as indeed your journey is long. Nothing is hidden from Allāh, neither in the heavens nor in the earth. Salām.

Al-Ghazālī said:

These reports and narrations indicate what is found in mixing with the leaders such as fitan and corruption. However, we will explain that in detail and understanding and distinguish what is prohibited from what is disliked and permitted. We say therefore: visiting the ruler is objectionable because he (the scholar visiting the ruler) disobeys Allāh, by his actions, by his silence, by his words, or by his belief which does not depart from one of these cases. As for via action: then this is by visiting them which in most instances is in a residence which has been usurped from someone else. Entering such a premises without the permission of the king is harām and being humble to an oppressor is not permitted except to only give salāms. As for kissing the hand of the ruler and bending over in servitude to him then this is disobedience. It has been relayed from some of the Salaf that they even prohibited returning salāms to the rulers and that one should turn away from them and have contempt for them as a virtuous good deed. As for sitting on the furniture of the rulers then if most of their wealth is from harām then it is impermissible to sit on their furniture.

As for remaining silent then this is in regards to seeing what is harām such as silk on the furniture, silver cutlery, silk clothing on them and their servants. Whoever sees anything evil and is silent about it is a partner in that evil. Rather, he even hears vile language from the rulers along with lying, slander and insults yet is silent about all of that – this is harām. If you say: "he fears for himself so he is thus excused for his silence" – then this is right however he is not sufficed from turning himself away from committing what is not permitted except with an excuse. If he did not enter the rulers' dwellings he would not have seen such evils and he would not be addressed to account for that, so his excuse is dropped from him. Whoever knows of corruption in a particular place and knows that he is unable to remove it, it is not permissible for him to attend such a place wherein he will see such corruption in front of him while he looks on and is silent, rather he is to protect himself from viewing such things.

As for by speech then this is when he supplicates for the ruler or praises him, or believes whatever clear falsehood he says. This affirmation of the rulers' falsehood could be via statement, nodding of the head, rejoicing in the leader's face, manifesting love and allegiance to the ruler, longing to meet the ruler, manifesting statements safeguarding that the ruler has a long life and lives long. In most cases he (the scholar who visits the ruler) will not be limited to just giving salāms rather he will speak with him with words which do not surpass other than the leader.

As for supplicating for the ruler he is visiting then this is not permitted except if he says: "may Allāh rectify you" or "may Allāh grant you success to goodness" or "may Allāh lengthen your life in doing obedience to Him", or similar such words. As for supplicating for him for the ruler to have control and live long and be blessed, along with words such as "master" and words which carry similar meaning – then this is not permissible. The Prophet ﷺ said: *"Whoever supplicates for an oppressor that he lives long has loved to disobey Allāh in His Earth."*[1] If he transgresses the bounds in

[1] Al-Hāfidh al-'Irāqī stated in his Takhrīj of *al-Ihyā'*, vol.2, p.88:

supplication and starts to praise him and mention that which is not true about him he becomes a liar or a Munāfiq or one who respects an oppressor. These three are all disobedient. The Prophet ﷺ: *"Allāh is angered if a fāsiq is praised."*[1] In another report: *"Whoever honours a*

I did not find this in marfū' form, it was only reported by Ibn Abi'd-Dunyā in *as-Samt*, it is of the statements of al-Hasan.

The author mentioned it in *Āfāt ul-Lisān* and in *as-Samt*, nos.230 and 600, the editor of it said: "The Shaykh, the classifier, deemed it weak as did al-Khatīb." Refer to adh-Dhahabī, *al-Mīzān* and as-Sakhāwī mentioned it under hadīth no. 1121 saying: "az-Zamakhsharī mentioned it in the tafsīr of Sūrat Hūd as did al-Ghazālī in two instances in *al-Ihyā'*." I did not see it in a *marfū'* form however it is at no.66 in *Shu'b ul-Īmān* by al-Bayhaqī and in *as-Samt* by Ibn Abi'd-Dunyā as being a statement of al-Hasan al-Basrī. This is how al-Ghazālī himself ascribed it in the third instance of it being found in *al-Ihyā'*. Abū Nu'aym reported it in the biography of ath-Thawrī in *al-Hilyah*. Ash-Shawkānī stated that it was fabricated in *al-Fawā'id al-Majmū'ah*, p.211. Refer to Ustādh Lutfī as-Sabāgh's commentary on *al-Asrār al-Marfū'ah*, pp.316-317.

[TN] *Kitāb us-Samt wa Adāb ul-Lisān* by Ibn Abi'd-Dunyā was edited by Najm 'AbdurRahmān Khalaf in 1986 and printed by Dār al-Gharb al-Islāmī in Beirut.

[1] Reported by Ibn Abi'd-Dunyā in *as-Samt*, no.229 from the hadīth of Anas and the editor of it said: "...the chain of transmission is weak." It is as he said, al-Huwaynī said: "the chain of transmission is very weak" and it was reported by Ibn Hibbān in *al-Majrūhīn*, vol.1, p.267, and Abū Ya'lā joined the report onto his Musnad as is mentioned in *al-Fath*, vol.10, p.478. This is relayed from Ibn Hibbān by Ibn 'Adiyy in *al-Kāmil*, vol.3, p.1307 and al-Khatīb in *at-Tārīkh*, vol.7, p.298, vol.8, p.428 via the route of Abū Khalaf from Anas. Al-Hāfidh stated in *al-Fath*, vol.10, p.278: "within the sanad is weakness." I say: this is *tasāhul* (leniency) as rather the sanad is

fāsiq, aids him in destroying Islām."[1] If this is surpassed by believing and affirming what the *fāsiq* says and commending him for what he does, then the person will be disobedient for the affirmation and the support (of the *fāsiq*). As for giving a commendation (to a *fāsiq*) or praising him then this is helping in disobedience and encouraging him to desire such disobedience. Just as denying him, censuring him and condemning him is an admonishment for him and a weakening of his actions. Helping in disobedience is disobedience even if it is by a small portion of a word. Sufyān was asked about an oppressor who is about to die out of thirst in the desert: "should water be brought

---

very weak. Al-Hāfidh stated in *at-Taqrīb* in the biography of Abū Khalaf: "He is Matrūk and Ibn Ma'īn accused him of lying." It has a supporting hadīth which is narrated by Buraydah which has been reported by Ibn 'Adiyy, vol.5, p.1917 via the route of 'Uqbah bin 'Abdullāh al-Asamm from 'Abdullāh bin Buraydah from his father in a marfū' form. 'Uqbah bin 'Abdullāh is a weak narrator.

I say (i.e. Abū 'Ali): al-'Irāqī stated in his *Takhrīj*, vol.2, p.88: "Reported by Ibn Abi'd-Dunyā in *as-Samt* and Ibn 'Adiyy in *al-Kāmil* and Abū Ya'lā and al-Bayhaqī from the hadīth of Anas with a weak chain of transmission." As-Sakhāwī weakened it in *al-Maqāsid*, p.412 and he ascribed it to al-Bayhaqī in *ash-Shu'b*.

[1] Al-'Irāqī stated in his Takhrīj of the *Ahādīth ul-Ihyā'*, vol.2, p.88: *Gharīb* with this wording and what is a well-known narration is: "whoever honours a person of innovation..." reported by Ibn 'Adiyy from the hadīth of 'Ā'ishah and reported by at-Tabarānī in *al-Awsat* and Abū Nu'aym in *al-Hilyah* from the hadīth of 'Abdullāh bin Busr with a da'īf chain of transmission. Ibn ul-Jawzī stated: "all of it is da'īf." Ash-Shawkānī stated in *al-Fawā'id*, p.211: "its isnad is da'īf" and Ibn ul-Jawzī stated: "it is fabricated."

for him?" Sufyān replied: "No, leave him to die as that will be helping him."

Also, he (who visits the ruler) will not be safe from the corruption which can reach his heart in multiple ways when he sees the vast blessings (that the ruler) has been bestowed with in comparison to what he has been given by Allāh and this is what Allāh's Messenger has forbade when he said ﷺ: "*O gathering of Muhājirīn, do not visit the people of the Dunyā for indeed it causes discontentment (Maskhata) with provision.*"[1] Such visitations are either disliked or prohibited and it is not permissible to enter the dwellings (of such people) except with two excuses:

Firstly: that the visit has been compelled and not merely out of honouring, and the visitor knows that if he does not go he will be harmed.

Secondly: that the visitor enters (the dwellings of the ruler) so as to avert transgression from a Muslim. There is a concession for this with the condition that the visitor does not lie, and he should not leave off giving advice he should rather anticipate that the advice will be accepted.

---

[1] I did not find this hadīth in my sources and al-Hāfidh al-'Irāqī did not discuss it in his takhrīf of *al-Ihyā'*, vol.2, p.13, rather he discussed aother hadīth relayed by al-Hākim which has been reported prior. I am still searching for this hadīth and whoever finds it can send it to me, may Allāh increase him in goodness.

Then al-Ghazālī states:

> And if you say: 'but the '*Ulama* from the Salaf used to visit the rulers', then I say: yes, learn how they visited them and then visit them! It was narrated that:[1] Hishām bin 'AbdulMalik had to go to Makkah and when he arrived there he said: "bring me a man from the Sahābah." It was said to him: "O leader of the believers, they have all passed away!" Hishām bin 'AbdulMalik replied: "Then bring me a man from the successors!" So then Tāwūs al-Yamānī[2] was

---

[1] In the margins of manuscript 'a' it reads: 'Tāwūs al-Yamānī Entering the Royal Quarters of Hishām bin 'AbdulMalik'.

[2] He is Tāwūs bin Kaysān, the outstanding jurist and scholar of Yemen, Abū 'AbdurRahmān, the Hāfidh. He was originally Persian and heard from Zayd bin Thābit, 'Ā'ishah, Abū Hurayrah and Ibn 'Abbās and he is of the senior companions of Ibn 'Abbās. Those who narrated from him were: 'Atā', Mujāhid, Ibn Shihāb, Abu'z-Zubayr al-Makkī and many others. Ibn 'Abbās said: "I consider Tāwūs as being from among the people of Jannah." Tāwūs was a scholar and stern practitioner of the truth, he was also trustworthy in narration. He died in 106 AH. For his biography refer to *Tabaqāt Ibn Sa'd*, vol.5, p.537; *at-Tārīkh al-Kabīr*, vol.4, p.365; *Tārīkh al-Fasawī*, vol.1, p.705; *al-Jarh wa't-Ta'dīl*, vol.4, p.500; *Hilyat ul-Awliyā'*, vol.4, pp.3-23; *Wafayāt ul-A'yān*, vol.2, p.509; *Tadhkirat ul-Huffādh*, vol.1, p.90; *al-'Ibar*, vol.1, p.130; *as-Siyar*, vol.5, pp.38-49; *Tahdhīb ut-Tahdhīb*, vol.5, p.8; *Tabaqāt ul-Huffādh*, p.34 and *Shadharāt udh-Dhahab*, vol.1, p.133.

[TN] It is unfortunate to see some of the Khawārij of the era, such as 'Abdullāh El-Faisal al-Jamaykī, disparage Tāwūs al-Yamānī. For Faisal stated after an hour and fifteen minutes into a lecture entitled *'Cancers in the Body of the Ummah'*:

summoned and when he entered (Hishām's dwellings) he removed his shoes, placed them next to the royal carpet and did not give salāms to him by addressing him as 'leader of the believers' rather he said: "Peace unto you O Hishām!" He did not address him by his *kunyah* and then sat down next to Hishām and said: "How are you O Hishām!" Hishām became very angry at this to the extent that he was going to kill Tāwūs.[1] Hishām said to Tāwūs: "What has led you to behave in this manner?!" Tāwūs replied "Why, what have I done?!" Hishām became even more angered and said: "You take off your shoes, place them next to the royal carpet, you did not even kiss my hand, you did not give salāms to me by addressing me as 'leader of the believers', you did not address me by my *kunyah*, then you came in and sat next to me without my permission and said 'how are you Hishām?'" Tāwūs replied by saying: "As for your saying 'You take off your shoes, place them next to the royal carpet' then I take them off five times everyday when I am in front of the Lord of the Worlds and He neither punishes me nor gets angry with me. As for your saying 'you did not even kiss my hand' then I heard 'Ali bin Abī

"The statement of kufr dūna kufr where did it come from? Qurtubi says it come *{sic}* from Tāwūs! A man who did not even meet the Prophet ﷺ, a man by the name of Tāwūs came up with this statement kufr dūna kufr. So as for the statement kufr dūna kufr Ibn 'Abbās did not make this statement!"

[1] In *al-Ithāf*, vol.6, p.138 is an addition: "...it was said to Tāwūs: 'you are in the sanctuary of Allāh and His Messenger.'"

Tālib say: 'It is not allowed for a man to kiss the hand of another except for his wife whom he kisses out of desire or his son who he kisses out of mercy.' As for your saying 'you did not give salāms to me by addressing me as 'leader of the believers'' then not everyone is pleased with your leadership and I hated to lie. As for your saying: 'you did not address me by my kunyah' then Allāh addressed His *Awliyā'* and said "O Dāwud",[1] "O Yahyā",[2] "O 'Īsā"[3] yet addressed His enemies by their kunyahs for Allāh says:

﴿ تَبَّتْ يَدَآ أَبِى لَهَبٍ وَتَبَّ ﴾

"May the hands of Abū Lahab be ruined, and ruined is he."

{al-Masad (111): 1}

As for your saying: 'then you came in and sat next to me without my permission' then I heard 'Ali ibn Abī Tālib say: 'If you want to look at a man from the people of Jahannam then look at a man who sits and around him are people standing." Hishām said: "Tāwūs has truly

---

[1] As in where Allāh says;

"...O David, indeed We have made you a successor upon the earth..."

{Sād (38): 26}

[2] As in where Allāh says;

"...O John, take the Scripture with determination."

{Maryam (19): 12}

[3] As in where Allāh says;

"...O Jesus, Son of Mary, remember My favor upon you and upon your mother..."

{al-Mā'idah (5): 110}

admonished me!" Tāwūs then said: "I heard 'Ali bin Abī Tālib say: 'In Jahannam are snakes the size of camels and scorpions the size of donkeys which bite the leader who was unjust with his populace.'" Then Tāwūs got up and left.

From Sufyān ath-Thawrī who said: "I visited Abū Ja'far in Mina and he said to me 'raise your need to me.' I said to him: 'Fear Allāh! For you have filled the earth with transgression and oppression.' Abū Ja'far bowed his head and then raised it saying: 'raise your need to us.' I (i.e. Sufyān) said: 'You gained this status due to the swords of the Muhājirīn and Ansār and now their children are dying of hunger. Fear Allāh and give them their rights!'"[1]

This is how they (the Salaf) used to enter (the quarters and dwellings) of the rulers, for they used to flee with their souls for the sake of Allāh, I am referring to the '*Ulama* of the hereafter. As for the *'Ulama* of the Dunyā [the scholars who desire the worldly life] then they enter the (quarters and dwellings) of the rulers in order to gain closeness to the rulers' hearts and thus make concessions for the rulers and make deductions via detailed tricks which agree with the rulers' own interests.

---

[1] An abridged version of the story via other routes of transmission have been reported by Abū Nu'aym in *al-Hilyah*, vol.6, p.377 and also mentioned by adh-Dhahabī in *as-Siyar*, vol.7, pp.262-263, pp.264-265.

Shaykh 'Izzaddīn bin 'AbdusSalām[1] stated in *Amālī*, which was commented upon by his student Shaykh Shihābuddīn al-Qarāfī,[2] one of the Mālikī Imāms:

> From what Shaykh 'Izzaddīn said ﵀, is that some state officials wrote to him exhorting him to meet up with the king of their era in order to increase his repute and suppress his political enemies. Shaykh 'Izzadīn wrote back to those officials saying: "I have studied knowledge so as to be an ambassador between Allāh and His creation, so how can I frequent the gates of those (rulers)?!" He indicated that whoever carries knowledge has become a transmitter from Allāh to His Servants in the status of messengership. Whoever

---

[1] The Sultān of the 'Ulama, al-'Allāmah, Shaykh 'Izzaddīn ibn 'AbdusSalām, and his name is 'Abdul'Azīz. He is of the senior Shāfi'ī scholars and one of their Mujtahid scholars. He was born in Damascus in 577 AH (1161 CE) and he has a number of situations with the rulers. Of his writings are: *Fawā'id ul-Hukkām fī Islāh il-Anām, Bidāyat us-Sūl* and other works. He died in 660 AH (1261 CE). For his biography refer to *Fawāt ul-Wafayāt*, vol.1, p.278; *Tabaqāt us-Subkī*, vol.5, p.80; az-Ziriklī, *al-A'lām*, vol.4, pp.144-145 and other sources.

[2] Ahmad bin Idrīs, well-known as Shihābuddīn, and he is of the senior Mālikī scholars and jurists. He was originally Persian and was born in Egypt where he was raised and where he also died. He has some good works in fiqh and usūl such as *al-Furūq, Tanqīh ul-Fusūl wa Sharhihi, adh-Dhakhīrah* (in fiqh). His students were: al-'Izz bin 'AbdusSalām. Al-Qarāfī died ﵀, in 684 AH. For his biography refer to: *ad-Dībāj*, pp.62-67; Muhammad Makhlūf, *Shajarat un-Nūr*, p.188; *al-A'lām*, vol.1, p.90 and other sources.

has this nobility it is not good for him to do that (frequent the gates and doors of the rulers).

Ibn ul-Hajj[1] stated in *al-Madkhal*:

> It is imperative for a scholar, rather it is an individual responsibility upon him, to not frequent the places of the children of the dunyā (i.e. the rulers) because the people have to be at the door of the scholar and not the other way round wherein the scholar is at the doors of the rulers. It is neither a proof for him that he (goes to the rulers because he) fears an enemy, an envious person or the like who can confuse him; nor that he hopes to avert something which he fears or hopes to fulfil the Muslims' needs so as to obtain a benefit for the Muslims, or avert a harm from them. However, these are not credible excuses for him. As for the first scenario (that he goes to the ruler out of fear) then if he does this out of Ishrāfu Nafs (blameworthy expectation of receiving gifts on account of visiting the ruler and feeling hurt and disappointed due to not getting anything)

---

[1] Muhammad bin Muhammad Abū 'Abdullāh al-'Abdarī al-Mālikī and he is considered one of the later Imāms of the Mālikī Madhhab. He is originally Persian and then lived in Egypt where he also died in 737 AH after living there for nearly eighty years. Of his works are: *al-Madkhal ila'sh-Shar' ash-Sharīf*, 4 vols., *al-Azhār at-Tayyibah an-Nashr* and other works. For his biography refer to *ad-Dībāj*, p.327; Ibn Hajar, *ad-Durar al-Kāminah*, vol.4, p.237; *al-A'lām*, vol.7, p.264 and other works.

then he will not be blessed in it. If he is fearful (of the ruler) then this is a better state than Ishrāfu Nafs (blameworthy expectation), because his being afflicted by a ruler who is hesitant in fulfilling Muslims' interest as an accelerated punishment for him.

As for the second scenario (visiting in order to gain a benefit for the Muslims or avert harm from them): then if he does this, he would have commited a verified prohibition just for a prohibition which may, or may not, possibly occur in the future (yet has not actually occurred as opposed to what has definitely occurred in the form of the prohibition of actually visiting the ruler). Hence, it is sought after at the time that he does not commit that censured action (of visiting the ruler) which is condemned in the Divine Legislation. Rather, assisting Muslims in getting their needs fulfilled is only achieved by cutting off from the gates of those rulers, having reliance solely on Allāh and returnng back to Allāh as He is the Fulfiller of needs, Averter of harms from the one in fear, Compeller of the creations' hearts Who makes them act as He wills and however He wills. Allāh says in addressing the master of creation (Muhammad ﷺ):

﴿ وَأَلَّفَ بَيْنَ قُلُوبِهِمْ ۚ لَوْ أَنفَقْتَ مَا فِى ٱلْأَرْضِ جَمِيعًا مَّآ أَلَّفْتَ بَيْنَ قُلُوبِهِمْ وَلَٰكِنَّ ٱللَّهَ أَلَّفَ بَيْنَهُمْ ۚ إِنَّهُۥ عَزِيزٌ حَكِيمٌ ﴾

"If you had spent all that is in the earth, you could not have brought their hearts together; but Allāh brought them together."

{al-Anfāl (8): 63}

Allāh mentions this when showing Imtinān (gratitude) to His Prophet ﷺ. The scholar, if he is one who follows the Prophet ﷺ especially in relying on His Lord and trusting Him as opposed to His creation, then Allāh will treat him with this kind treatment with which He treated the Prophet ﷺ as a blessing of following the Prophet ﷺ; and with that that he is saved from frequenting the doors of those rulers as is done by some people, and it is a lethal poison.

Would that they restricted themselves to what has been mentioned here and nothing more, yet rather they join onto that something which is more severe and reprehsible which is that they say their frequenting the doors of the rulers is out of humbleness or out of guiding the rulers to good, and other reasons which are dangerous to them and which greatly cause widespread problems. If these scholars believe that then the hope of them repenting and retracting (from their action of frequenting the gates of the rulers) is decreased. Some of our *'Ulama* have transmitted that if an honest and credible person of good repute frequents the door of the judge then this tarnishes his reputation and leads to his testimony being rejected. So if this is just in regards to frequenting the door of the judge, and is done by a Muslim scholar who leaves his gathering to go to the gathering of those (judges), then what about frequenting the doors of those other than the judge? It takes precedence and is more obligatory to prohibit that.

Then Ibn ul-Hajj stated in another instance:

> It is incumbant on the scholar that when his fixed due provision for teaching is cut off from him that he does not abandon the *ijtihād* that he was involved in and he does not give up. He does not give up because his provision could have been cut off from him as a test from Allāh in order for Allāh to see the scholar's truthfulness in knowledge and action. For his provision is guaranteed to him and is not confined to only one direction (from where it comes). The Prophet ﷺ said: *"Whoever seeks knowledge, Allāh will be responsible for providing for him."*[1] This means: Allāh will make it easy for him without any tiredness or difficulty. Even though Allāh takes responsibility of all of the creations' provisions He specifies mentioning that in regards to the scholar Allāh will make it easy for

[1] Reported by al-Khatīb al-Baghdādī in *Tārīkh Baghdād*, vol.3, p.180 and al-Khatīb stated: "of the Gharīb hadīth narrated by ath-Thawrī from his father from his grandfather , I do not know its narrators except for Yūnus bin 'Atā'." Ibn Hibbān said: "Yūnus bin 'Atā' narrates strange things, it is not permitted to utilise his rcports." Al-Hākim, an-Naqqāsh and Abū Nu'aym said: "he reported fabricated narrations from Humayd at-Tawīl." See Ibn Hajar, *Lisān ul-Mīzān*, vol.6, pp.406-407. The hadīth is found in al-Albānī's *Da'īf ul-Jāmi'*, no.5684 and al-Albānī said about it: "fabricated."

him without tiredness or difficulty and makes his portion of tiredness and difficulty in teaching, investigating and understanding issues and delivering them. This treatment towards him from Allāh is out of kindness to the scholar and being good to him and it is also of the supernatural wonders of the *'Ulama,* I mean: understanding issues and then being able to deliver the issues onto others in a good way, along with knowledge of people's dispositions in learning the issues. Just as the supernatural wonders of the Awliyā' include other things which are too numerous to enumerate such as walking on water, flying in the air etc. (by Allah's permission).

The scholar has to preserve this noble position from frequenting those who can assist in releasing the due provision, or from speaking about it or from seeking a replacement for this provision. One who I trust has narrated to me that he saw a scholar teaching in a school and then his due provision was cut off from him and his students. The students on one occasion asked a scholar who had this done to him: "maybe you should go to so-and-so (from the rulers)! Meet him and he will maybe instruct for the provision to be released." The scholar replied: "By Allāh, I feel ashamed in front of my Lord ﷻ, this old man is denied by him." The students replied: "how is this?!" The scholar said: "I get up everyday and I say: 'O Allāh there is no preventer of what You have given and there is no giver of what You have prevented.'[1] I say this, so how can I stand in front of the creation and ask him for that?! By Allāh I will not do so."

The scholar is the first one who should place trust in his Lord ﷻ, in regards to preventing and giving sustenance and provision, and he has no excuse in seeking provision. This is because Allāh's intent with thc *'Ulama* is that they resort to Him and rely on Him in all of their affairs without looking at the reasons or the Causer and Arranger of the affairs Who is Ever-Able over the affairs. How can this not be the case when then scholar is the one who guides the creation and clarifies the straight way to Allāh. Whoever leaves something for the sake of Allāh, Allāh will replace it with something better from where he does not expect.[2]

---

[1] Inferring the hadīth which is reported by al-Bukhārī and Muslim from al-Mughīrah bin Shu'bah that Allāh's Messenger ﷺ use to say after every Salāh: "*La ilaha il Allahu wahdahu la sharika lahu; lahu'l-mulk wa lahu'l-hamd, wahuwa ala kulli shay'in qadir. Allahumma la mani'a Lima a'taita, wa la mu'tia Lima mana'ta, wa la yanfa'u dhal-jaddu minkal-jadd.*"

[2] Inferring to a da'īf hadīth which is no authentic, refer to as-Sakhawī, *al-Maqāsid al-Hasanah*, no.949.

[TN] I have slightly abridged this quote from Ibn ul-Hajj ﷺ as relayed from Imām as-Suyūtī.

In *Tabaqāt ul-Hanafiyyah* it is relayed in the biography of 'Ali bin al-Hasan as-Sandalī:[1]

> The ruler King Shāh said about him: "you did not come to me?!" As-Sandalī replied: "I wanted you to be from the best of kings who visit the *'Ulama*, and I did not want to from the most evil 'Ulama who visit kings."

Ibn 'Adiyy[2] stated in *al-Kāmil*:

> I heard Abu'l-Husayn Muhammad bin al-Mudhaffar[3] say: I heard our *Mashā'iykh* in Egypt attest to the virtue of Abū 'AbdurRahmān

---

[1] 'Ali bin al-Husayn bin 'Ali Abu'l-Mahāsin an-Naysabūrī, he was an Imām and a scholar who read to al-Husayn bin 'Ali as-Sumayrī from Abū Bakr Muhammad al-Khawārizmī from al-Jassās from al-Barda'ī from Mūsā bin Nasr from Muhammad. He authored *Tafsīr ul-Qur'ān* and he died in 484 AH. 'Ali al-Qārī mentioned that he had a role in speaking against the Mu'tazilah. He travelled to Baghdad with the ruler and then when he returned to Naysabūr he cut off from the ruler, became ascetic and did not visit the rulers, hence this story. It was said about him that: '...he used to practice the Sunnah in his clothing, he strove to walk to Jumu'ah and he gave salāms to all who passed by him.' Abridged from al-Hāfidh al-Qurashī, *al-Jawāhir al-Mad'iyyah*, vol.1, p.357; al-Luknowī, *al-Fawā'id al-Bahiyyah*, p.120 and *al-A'lām*, vol.5, pp.81-82.

[2] In manuscript 'a': 'Abū 'Adiyy'.

[3] A Muhaddith and Hāfidh, he was born in 286 AH and died in 379 AH, for his biogrphy refer to *Tadhkirat ul-Huffādh*, vol.3, pp.980-983 and also see the margins of *as-Siyar*, vol.16, p.418.

an-Nasā'ī[1] in regards to his advancement and leadership. They described his determination in worship throughout the night and his diligence in *ijtihād*, and that he went out to battle with the ruler of Egypt. An-Nasā'ī was described on account of his shahāmah (chivalry), practice of the Sunan inherited from the Prophet ﷺ and his precaution against sitting with the Sultān with whom he did battle. This was his habit until he was martyred ﷺ.[2]

In al-Mizzī's *Tahdhīb ul-Kamāl,* with his chain of transmission from Rushdayn bin Sa'd who said:

---

[1] Ahmad bin Shu'ayb an-Nasā'ī, the Imām, Hāfidh, Shaykh ul-Islām, an-Nāqid al-Kabīr. He was born in Nasā (in Khurasān) in the year 215 AH. He heard from many such as Ishāq bin Rāhawayh, Hishām bin 'Ammār, al-Hārith bin Miskīn and from many other whom he travelled to and heard from. Those who narrated from him include: ad-Dūlābī, at-Tahāwī, Ibn us-Sunnī and a large body of others. Adh-Dhahabī stated about him: "He was of the oceans of knowledge, possessed understanding, precision, insight, criticism of narrators and good authorship." He died ﷺ in the year 303 AH. For his biography refer to *Wafayāt ul-A'yān*, vol.1, pp.77-78; *Tahdhīb ul-Kamāl*, vol.1, pp.23-25; *Tadhkirat ul-Huffādh*, vol.2, pp.698-701; *as-Siyar*, vol.14, pp.125-135; *Tabaqāt ush-Shāfi'iyyah*, vol.3, pp.14-16; *al-Bidāyah wa'n-Nihāyah*, vol.11, pp.123-124; *Tahdhīb ut-Tahdhīb*, vol.1, pp.36-37; *Shadharāt udh-Dhahab*, vol.2, pp.239-241 and other sources.

[2] I did not find this within *al-Kāmil* rather I came across it in al-Hāfidh al-Mizzī's *Tahdhīb ul-Kamāl*, vol.1, p.23 and likewise in a route of transmission of al-Hākim. This is what is mentioned by adh-Dhahabī in *as-Siyar*, vol.14, pp.131-132.

I heard Ibrāhīm bin Adham[1] say: I heard that: '...the most honoured of things towards the end of time are three: a brother for the sake of Allāh; earning a Dirham from that which is halāl and speaking a true word with a ruler (Sultān).'[2]

---

[1] Abū Ishāq Ibrāhīm bin Adham al-'Iljī, the fine Imām and Zāhid. He narrated from al-A'mash, Abū Ishāq as-Subay'ī and Mālik bin Dīnār. Those who narrated from him were: ath-Thawrī, Shaqīq al-Balkhī, al-Farīyābī (who was from Farīyāb, a town between Balkh and Marw ar-Rud) and others. An-Nasā'ī said about him: "He is trustworthy and safe, one of the ascetics." He died ﷺ in the year 162 AH. For his biography refer to *at-Tārīkh al-Kabīr*, vol.1, p.273; *al-Jarh wa't-Ta'dīl*, vol.2, p.87; *Hilyat ul-Awliyā'*, vol.7, p.367 and vol.8, p.58; as-Siyar, vol.7, pp.387-396; *al-Bidāyah wa'n-Nihāyah*, vol.10, pp.135-145; *Tahdhīb ut-Tahdhīb*, vol.1, pp.102-103; *Shadharāt udh-Dhahab*, vol.1, pp.255-256 and other sources.

[2] [TN] It has been reported that the Prophet ﷺ said: "*From the Greatest acts of Jihad is to say a just word to an oppressive ruler.*" This hadīth is used by many *takfīrīs* today to justify their public ramblings about Muslim rulers and Islamic and political matters of which they know very little. Moreover, the hadīth is in fact unreliable; our Shaykh Mashūr Āl Salmān stated:

> This is reported by at-Tirmidhī in his *Jaami'* (no. 2174); Abū Dāwud in his *Sunan* (no. 4344); Ibn Mājah in his *Sunan* (no. 4011); al-Khateeb in his *Tārīkh* (vol.7, p.238); al-Mizzī in *Thadheeb ul-Kāmil* (vol.17, p.405) via 'Atiyyah al-'Awfī from Abū Sa'eed al-Khudrī. In Abū Dāwud and al-Khateeb it has the addition of "or an oppressive leader ('Ameer)". At-Tirmidhī stated "*The hadīth is hasan ghareeb from this angle*" and 'Atiyyah is: Ibn Sa'd Ibn Janādah who is *sudūq* but makes many mistakes and he was a Shī'ah and a Mudallis, as al-Hāfidh stated in *at-Taqreeb* (4616).[2]

[End of Treatise]

Az-Zabīdī further said about him, "*In fact 'Atiyyah was weakened before his practice of Tadlees and becoming a Shī'ī.*" See *Itihāf us-Sa'ādat il-Muttaqeen bi Sharh Asrār Ihyā 'Ulūm id-Deen* [Gifting the Happiness of the Pious with an Explanation of the Secrets of Ihyā 'Ulūm ud-Deen] (Cairo: Matba'ah al-Maymaniyyah, 1311 AH/1893 CE and Beirut: Dār ul-Kutub il-'Ilmiyyah, 1989 CE – edited by R. 'AbdulHaadī) vol.5, p.88. Furthermore, Adh-Dhahabī said:

> "*Imām Ahmad, an-Nasā'ī and a group of other scholars said about him to be weak and Salim al-Muradī said about 'Atiyyah that he was a Shi'ite.*"

See *Mīzān al-I'tidāl* vol.3, p.79, *Tahdheeb at-Tahdeeb*, vol.7, p.224. In *al-Adhkār* p.58, 'chapter: what to say when entering the mosque', an-Nawawī mentions the above report through two different chain of narrators and states that in the first chain one finds Wāzih ibn Nāfi' al-Aqīlī, about whom there is an *ijma* on his weakness, and in the second chain one finds 'Atiyyah al-'Awfī who is also weak. Al-Hāfidh al Mundhirī also declared 'Attiyah to be weak in *at-Targheeb* vol.3, p.459. Note: There are also some *hadīth* which are used to justify *tawassul* which feature 'Atiyyah al-'Awfī in the *sanad* such as: "*The one who leaves his house for prayer and then says: O Allah, I ask you by the right of those who ask you and I beseech you by the right of those who walk this path unto you.*"

Bibliography

Al-Ājurrī, *Akhlāq ul-'Ulama* (Morocco: Dār uth-Thaqāfah, 1984 CE, ed. Fārūq Hamādah).

'Abbās, Ihsān: *Rasā'il Ibn Hazm al-Andalūsī* (Beirut: al-Mu'assisat ul-'Arabiyyah li-d-Dirasāt wa'n-Nashr, 1987).

Al-'Ajlūnī, *Kashf ul-Khifā'* (Beirut).

Al-Alā'ī, *Jāmi' ut-Tahsīl* (Baghdād: Wizārat ul-Awqāf, 1978, ed. Hamdī 'AbdulHamīd as-Salafī).

Al-Albānī, *Sahīh ul-Jāmi' al-Kabīr* (Beirut: al-Maktab al-Islāmī, 1982).

Al-Albānī, *Da'īf ul-Jāmi' as-Saghīr* (Beirut: al-Maktab al-Islāmī, 1988)

Al-Albānī, *Sahīh ul-Jāmi' as-Saghīr* (Beirut: al-Maktab al-Islāmī, 1982).

Al-Albānī, *Sahīh ut-Targhīb wa't-Tarhīb* (Beirut: al-Maktab al-Islāmī, 1986).

Al-Albānī, *Silsilat ul-Ahādīth as-Sahīhah* (al-Maktab al-Islāmī, 1983)

Al-Albānī, *Silsilat ul-Ahādīth ad-Da'īfah* (Riyadh: al-Maktab al-Islāmī wa'l-Ma'ārif, 1988)

Al-Asfahānī, Abū Nu'aym: *Hilyat ul-Awliyā'* (Beirut: Dār ul-Kitāb al-'Arabī, 3rd Print, 1980 CE).

Al-Asnawī, *Tabaqāt ush-Shāfi'iyyah* (Baghdad: 1391 AH, ed. 'Abdullāh al-Jabūrī).

Badrān, *Tahdhīb Tārīkh Dimashq* (Damascus: 1329-1332 AH, ed. Rawdat ush-Shām).

Al-Baghdādī, al-Khatīb: *Iqtidā ul'Ilm bi'l-'Amal* (Beirut: al-Maktab al-Islāmī, ed. Al-Albānī).

Al-Baghdādī, al-Khatīb: *Tārīkh Baghdad* (Cairo: 1931 CE).

Al-Bayhaqī, *Shu'b ul-Eemān* (Beirut: Dār ul-Kutub al-'Ilmiyyah, 1990, ed. Bisyūnī Zaghlūl).

Al-Bukhārī, *at-Tārīkh al-Kabīr* (Beirut: Copy from the Indian Print).

Ad-Dabbī, *Bughyat ul-Multamis* (Egypt: Dār ul-Kitāb al-'Arabī, 1967 CE).

Ad-Dānī, Abū 'Amru: *as-Sunan al-Wāridah fi'l-Fitan* (manuscript within the Dhāhiriyyah Library, manuscript no.1105).

Ad-Daylamī *Firdaws ul-Akhbār* (Beirut: Dār ul-Kutub al-'Ilmiyyah, ed. Bisyūnī Zaghlūl).

Adh-Dhahabī, *al-'Ibar fī Khabar min Ghabar* (Kuwait, eds. Salāhuddīn al-Munajjid and Fu'ad as-Sayyid).

Adh-Dhahabī, *Tadhkirat ul-Huffādh* (Beirut: Dār Ihyā' ut-Turāth al-'Arabī, 1399 AH, ed. Al-Mu'allimī).

Adh-Dhahabī, *Duwal Islām* (Cairo: 1974 CE, eds. Fahīm Muhammad Shaltūt and Muhammad Mustafā Ibrāheem).

Adh-Dhahabī, *Siyar A'lām un-Nubalā'* (Beirut: Mu'assasat ur-Risālah, 1986 CE, eds. Shu'ayb al-Arna'ūt and et al.).

Al-Ghazālī, *Ihyā' 'Ulūm ud-Dīn* (Egypt, ed. 'Eesā al-Bābī al-Halabī).

Al-Haythamī, *Kashf ul-Astār* (Beirut: Mu'assasat ur-Risālah, 1979 CE, ed. Habīb ur-Rahmān al-A'dhamī).

Al-Hindī, al-Muttaqī, *Kanz ul-'Ummāl* (Beirut: Mu'assasat ur-Risālah, 1979).

Al-Hūt, *Asnā ul-Matālib* (Beirut).

Al-Humaydī, *Jadhwat ul-Muqtabis* (ad-Dār al-Misriyyah li't-ta'līf wa't-Tarjamah, 1966 CE)

Ibn ul-Athīr 'Izzaddīn, *Asad ul-Ghābah* (Cairo: 1970).

Ibn 'AbdulBarr, *al-Istīāb* (Cairo, ed. 'Ali al-Bajāwī).

Ibn 'AbdulBarr, *Jāmi' Bayān al-'Ilm wa Fadlihi* (Beirut: Dār ul-Fikr).

Ibn Abi'd-Dunyā, *as-Samt* (Beirut: Dār ul-Kutub al-'Ilmiyyah)

Ibn Abī Hātim ar-Rāzī, *'Ilal ul-Hadīth* (Beirut, Dār ul-Ma'rifah)

Ibn Abī Hātim ar-Rāzī, *al-Jarh wa't-Ta'deel* (Indian Print, 1373 AH)

Ibn 'Adiyy, *al-Kāmil fi'd-Du'afā'* (Beirut: Dār ul-Fikr, 1985 CE).

Ibn Bashkuwāl, *as-Sillah* (Cairo: 1966).

Ibn Dayba', *Tamyīz at-Tayyib min al-Khabīth* (Beirut: Dār ul-Kutub al-'Arabī).

Ibn Farhūn, ad-Dībāj ul-Madhhab (Egypt: Dār ut-Turāth, ed. Muhammad al-Ahmadī Abu'n-Nūr).

Ibn Hajar, *al-Isābah* (Cairo and Beirut, 1964, ed. Mawlay 'AbdulHafīdh).

Ibn Hajar, *Tabaqāt ul-Mudallisīn* (Jordan: Maktabat ul-Manār, 1988 CE, ed. 'Āsim al-Qaryūtī).

Ibn Hajar, *Taqrīb ut-Tahdhīb* (Beirut: Dār ul-Ma'rifah, 1975 CE, ed. 'AbdulWahhāb 'AbdulLatīf).

Ibn Hajar, *Tahdhīb ut-Tahdhīb* (Egypt: Dār ul-Kitāb al-Islāmī).

Ibn Hibbān, *Rawdat ul-'Uqalā'* (Beirut: Dār ul-Kutub al-'Ilmiyyah, 1977 CE, ed. Muhammad Muhyuddīn 'AbdulHamīd).

Ibn ul-'Imād al-Hanbalī, *Shadharāt udh-Dhahab* (Egypt and Beirut: al-Qudsī, 1350 AH).

Ibn Iyyās, *Badā'i uz-Zuhūr* (Cairo: 1311 AH).

Ibn ul-Jazarī, *Ghāyat ul-Nihāyah fee Tabaqāt il-Qurā'* (Cairo: 1932, ed. Gotthelf Bergstrasser).

Ibn Kathīr, *al-Bidāyah wa'n-Nihāyah* (Cairo and Beirut: 1358 AH).

Ibn Kathīr, *Tafsīr al-Qur'ān al-'Adhīm* (Beirut: Dār ul-Fikr).

Ibn Tāhir al-Hindī, *Tadhkirat ul-Mawdū'āt* (Beirut: Dār Ihyā' ut-Turāth al-'Arabī)

Jabūr, Jibrā'īl: *al-Kawākib us-Sā'irah* (Beirut).

Al-Jarrāh, Wakī' bin: *az-Zuhd* (ad-Dārat us-Sa'udiyyah, ed.'AbdurRahmān al-Farīwā'ī).

Khalīfah, Hijjī: *Kashf udh-Dhunūn* (Istanbul, 1941 CE).

Khan, Siddīq Hasan: *at-Tāj ul-Mukallal* (Beirut).

Al-Mizzī, *Tahdhīb ul-Kamāl* (Copied from original manuscript and published by Dār ul-Ma'mūn in Damascus).

Al-Mubārakfūrī, *Tuhfat ul-Ahwadhī* (Beirut: Dār ul-Fikr).

Al-Mundhirī, *at-Targhīb wa't-Tarhīb* (Beirut).

An-Nawawī, *Tahdhīb ul-Asmā' wa'l-Lughāt* (Cairo).

Al-Qādī 'Iyyād, *Tartīb ul-Madārik* (Beirut: Maktabat ul-Hayāh, ed. Ahmad Bakīr).

Al-Qafatī, *Inbā ur-Ruwāt* (Cairo: 1955 CE, ed. Muhammad Abu'l-Fadl Ibrāhīm).

Al-Qurashī, *al-Jawāhir al-Madiyyah* (Hyderabad, 1332 AH).

Ash-Shawkānī, *al-Badr at-Tāli'* (Cairo: 1348 AH).

Ash-Shawkānī, *al-Fawā'id ul-Majmū'ah* (Dār ul-Kutub al-'Ilmiyyah, ed. Al-Mu'allimī).

As-Sirrī, Hannād bin: *az-Zuhd* (ed. 'Abdurrahmān al-Fareewā'ī).

As-Subkī, *Tabaqāt ush-Shāfi'iyyah* (Cairo: 1976 CE, eds. 'AbdulFattāh al-Hilw and Mahmūd at-Tanāhī).

Sunan Abū Dāwud (Beirut: al-Maktabah al-'Asriyyah, ed. Muhammad Muhyuddīn 'AbdulHamīd, n.d.)

Sunan al-Bayhaqī (Beirut: Dār ul-Fikr, n.d.)

Sunan ad-Dārimī (Beirut: Dār ul-Kitaab al-'Arabī, 1987 CE, eds. Fu'ād Ahmad Zumarlī and Khālid as-Sab al-'Ulaymī)

Sunan Ibn Mājah (Beirut: Dār Ihyā ut-Turāth al-'Arabī, ed. Fu'ād AbdulBāqī, n.d.)

Sunan at-Tirmidhī (Beirut: Dār Ihyā ut-Turāth al-'Arabī, eds. Ahmad Muhammad Shākir et al., n.d.)

Sunan an-Nasā'ī (Beirut: Dār Ihyā ut-Turāth al-'Arabī, n.d.)

As-Suyūtī, *Husn ul-Muhādharah* (Cairo: 1387 AH, ed. Muhammad Abu'l-Fadl Ibrāhīm)

As-Suyūtī, *Tabaqāt ul-Huffādh* (Egypt: Maktabah Wahbah, 1973 CE).

As-Suyūtī, *Tahdhīr ul-Khuwwās* (al-Maktab al-Islāmī, 1984 CE, 2nd Edition, ed. Muhammad Lutfī as-Sabāgh).

Al-'Umarī, Akram Diyā: *Tabaqāt Khalīfah* (Riyadh: Tayyibah, 1982 CE).

Al-'Uqaylī, *ad-Du'afā al-Kabīr* (Beirut: Dār ul-Kutub al-'Ilmiyyah, 1984 CE, ed. 'AbdulMu'tī Qal'ajī).

Az-Zabīdī, *Ithāf us-Sādat il-Mutaqqīn* (Beirut: Dār ul-Fikr).

Az-Zabīdī, *Tabaqātun-Nahwiyyīn* (Cairo: 1954).

Az-Ziriklī, *al-A'lām* (Beirut: Dār ul-'Ilm li'l-Malāyīn, 1980).

JAMIAH MEDIA PUBLICATIONS

Previous Publications:

1. *Before Nicea.* By AbdurRahman Bowes and AbdulHaq al-Ashanti (2005)
2. *Who's in for Iraq?* By Shaykh Abdul'Azeez bin Rayyis ar-Rayyis (2007)
3. *The Impact of Man-Made Laws in the Ruling of an Abode as Being One of Kufr or Islam.* By Shaykh Khalid al-Anbari.(2006)
4. *A Warning Against Extremism.* By Shaykh Salih Aali Shaykh (2008)
5. *A Critical Study of the Multiple Identities and Disguises of 'al-Muhajiroun'.* By Abu Ameenah AbdurRahman as-Salafi and AbdulHaq al-Ashanti (2009).
6. *The Noble Women Scholars of Hadīth.* By Shaykh Mashhur Hasan Al Salman. (2010)
7. *The Creed of Imam an-Nawawi,* By Shaykh Mashhur Hasan Al Salman (2010)
8. *The Beautiful Advice to the Noble Salafis of the West,* By Shaykh 'Abdul-Aziz ar-Rayyis (2010)
9. *Shirk According to the 4 Madhhabs.* By Shaykh, Dr Muhammad al-Khumayyis. (2011)
10. *What the Notables Have Narrated About not Going to the Rulers,* Imam Jalalud-Deen as-Suyuti (2011)

11. *'Abdullah el-Faisal al-Jamayki' – A Critical Study of his Statements, Errors and Extremism in Takfir*, By Abu Ameenah AbdurRahman as-Salafi and AbdulHaq al-Ashanti (2011).

Forthcoming Publications:

12. *Guidance on the Ruling on Giving the Khutbah in a Non-Arabic Language.* By Abu Najeed Isam bin Ahmad Saleem bin Mami al-Makki

13. *The Fiqh Madhhab of Ahl ul-Hadith.* By Shaykh Mashhur Hasan Al Salman